HOW TO RAISE ENTREPRENEURIAL KIDS

Raising confident, resourceful
and resilient children who
are ready to succeed in life

JODIE COOK AND DANIEL PRIESTLEY

R^ethink

First published in Great Britain in 2020
by Rethink Press (www.rethinkpress.com)

Cover image © Shutterstock | zizi_mentos
Cover artwork background © Sam Moore
Cartoons © Andrew Priestley

CONTENTS

PREFACE

JODIE

It began in 2012. I was around a long boardroom table in London at a plush Mayfair office, with eleven other entrepreneurs. We were aged between twenty-two and thirty-one and our businesses were very different, but considerably successful. We had each started our ventures with less than £1,000 and we were around that table because we had been invited to be ambassadors of a government loans programme for start-ups. The loans offered by the programme were small, so our stories would be showcased as proof that it was possible to start and grow a business regardless of capital.

The discussion was chaired by James Caan, businessman and former *Dragons' Den* dragon. As we went around the table, each entrepreneur was invited to tell their story. Tales included the setup journey, the size of the business, how each company served its customers and the people it hired. When my turn came, I told the room I was one year into running my social media agency and had just hired my first two team members. I had the smallest business in the room at the time. Many of the others owned seriously impressive companies.

After hearing from everyone, a noticeably impressed James Caan asked the group, 'Out of interest, out of the twelve of you, who has a parent who also started their own business?' I put my hand up, because my mum had been self-employed for fifteen years. I remembered her starting her marketing consultancy after leaving the corporate world when I was at school.

I expected there might be one or two others with a similar experience, but to my shock I looked around the room and saw eleven of the twelve people with their hands up. Eleven out of twelve.

As we stared at each other around the table, in awe at what we had just uncovered, I realised that what made this remarkable was that it wasn't about money. We were there because we'd started our businesses with less than a thousand pounds. It had to be something else.

This encounter sparked the start of my journey delving into the influences that create entrepreneurs. A year into my business, I was aware that no one else I knew from school had set up on their own. They were mainly in higher education or climbing the corporate ladder. I didn't know if that's what they wanted for themselves, and I got the feeling they didn't know either.

I would meet people who truly believed they could never start their own business, or ask for a promotion, or set ambitious goals and work to achieve them. They believed that success and doing purposeful work were out of the question for their journeys. They underestimated themselves. They shied away from achieving or from doing what they actually wanted to do. It made no sense.

My research from that point led me to view *role models* as the overarching factor that influences someone to believe they can become an entrepreneur. Kids that have an entrepreneurial role model believe it's possible for them. Kids that don't, don't. Simple. While I know now that there's more to it, at the time it was the focus.

I brought my husband on board with the mission, and we embarked upon creating entrepreneurial role models for kids in the form of storybooks. We knew nothing about publishing or selling books, but at each stage our motto became, 'How hard can it be?' Writing a book? Sure. Finding an illustrator, editor, printer? Easy. Selling them in stores and on Amazon? Getting them into every school in the UK? No problem.

We wanted to create relatable role models who readers could be inspired by and emulate if they didn't have an entrepreneurial role model in their parents. We wanted the books to develop the behaviour and mindset associated with entrepreneurship so that the readers would see it as a viable option for their future. The books were fictional stories, not manuals on how to start a business. They led by example rather than instruction.

Four storybooks, a teacher's guide and an activity pack later, the mission was resonating with an audience. We had sold 100,000 copies. We were onto something. In the feedback from parents, which we received regularly, they described reading our books as 'flicking a switch' in the minds of their children. They said they had watched their kids go from letting problems defeat them to seeing obstacles as fun challenges to overcome. While they might once have complained of boredom, now they had plenty of ideas for what they could do.

The story-bound role models were doing their job. The books were creating behavioural change like positivity, creativity, resourcefulness and resilience – the key traits of entrepreneurs.

The support for the Clever Tykes storybooks has been astounding. Continued feedback from parents and educators of six- to nine-year-olds noticing positive changes in their children's behaviour since reading the books led me to believe there was more we could do.

In 2018, while conducting research for an article on raising entrepreneurial kids, I asked our audience two questions:

- 🚀 How are you raising entrepreneurial kids?

- 🚀 How were you raised to be entrepreneurial?

I also added the questions to Help a Reporter Out (HARO), thinking I might receive a few more responses. What followed was 500 responses from people sharing their stories. I spent weeks poring over these to discover their secrets.

The stories were incredible. The contributors were from different backgrounds and from all over the world. Each answer contained a detailed insight, a moving account or posed a different way of thinking about something. They all expressed intense gratitude towards the role models on their journey, parents or otherwise. Most importantly, they told stories with actionable messages. For many of the responses, it was almost as if the writers were having realisations as they were typing. 'Oh, there was that thing!' 'Oh, and this too!'

Some of the stories had parallels with my own journey. I thought back to growing up with a fierce sense of independence. My mum would encourage me to do things for myself. To work out the right answer and give it a go. I was packing my own suitcase for trips by the time I was four. I was making my own dentist and doctor's appointments by the time I was seven. Perhaps I was subconsciously raised to be entrepreneurial. Perhaps my story held secrets, too.

At that moment I realised that my flooded inbox possibly contained one of the deepest, most diverse and personal collections of entrepreneurial education that had ever existed. Right there, in 500 emails, we had not only the answer to how entrepreneurs all over the world were raised. They also contained the methods by which we could raise the entrepreneurs of the future. This was big.

The submissions I had were way too much for a blog post. They marked the start of a movement, and a significant contribution to the discussions surrounding this field. They had to be a book, and I knew exactly the person to bring on board. I was in Stockholm, Sweden when I called Daniel to pitch my idea. As soon as I said, 'How to raise entrepreneurial kids,' he replied, 'I'm in. What do you need?'

Daniel was the perfect partner for this book for several reasons. His entrepreneurial accelerator has worked with 3,000 entrepreneurs. He's written four books on the entrepreneurial journey and he's raising three kids of his own. He's consciously thinking, from a parent's point of view, of the effect that everything he says or does has on his kids.

I knew that combining this with my research and insights from entrepreneurs, parents and teachers would create a book containing ideas that would spread. It's a concept I've been fascinated with since 2012, and I know from my own journey what a difference it can make to someone's future. I will forever be grateful to my parents for equipping me to confidently make my own decisions, set my own goals and overcome challenges thrown at me, whatever they might be.

I'm convinced that the solution to raising aspirations and equipping the entrepreneurs and leaders of the future with the traits described above is in sharing the methods by which entrepreneurs are raised. We can't control someone's background but we can use education to level the playing field and ensure someone's past doesn't dictate their future. I hope you love this book.

UNITED NATIONS ALIGNMENT

In 2015, the United Nations created seventeen sustainable development goals for a better world by 2030.

This book proudly supports three of those goals:

- 🚀 **Goal number 4:** quality education
- 🚀 **Goal number 8:** decent work and economic growth
- 🚀 **Goal number 10:** reduced inequalities

This book is dedicated to Jodie's family:
Ben, Carol, Paul, Lucy and Nav;
and Daniel's family:
Aléna, Xander, Ethan and Isla;
and to his parents Andrew and Diane.

INTRODUCTION

DANIEL

There are kids that grow up ready to take on the world. They have the attitude, the skills and can spot opportunities that are right for them. They are excited about life – they are prepared and know they will handle whatever life throws their way.

These kids were lucky to have parents or guardians who gave them a balance of support and challenges, encouragement and discipline, learning and experience. These kids had parents who were part mentor and part coach – parents who helped them make sense of the world and instilled strong principles to guide them through life as young adults.

More than ever, kids with successful futures ahead of them are exposed to ideas normally associated with entrepreneurship. Entrepreneurs require creativity, empathy, communication skills, problem-solving abilities, practical mathematics and a knack for spotting opportunities at the right moment and having the confidence to act on them.

Raising a child with an awareness of entrepreneurship and the associated skills can change their life for the better even if they don't go on to start or scale a business. At the least, the same set of skills will steer them towards opportunities that are right for them.

Raising children and preparing them for life used to be simple. Teaching them good manners. Reading, writing and arithmetic at school. How to dress for a job interview and how to look someone in the eye and offer a firm handshake. Covering these basics was adequate for a world where people had clear career paths, rarely moved from their hometowns, married young, could afford a mortgage and had no need to worry about their industry changing rapidly.

Essentially, in years gone by if you got your child 'on the ladder' they would be perfectly capable of climbing the rungs on their own. Children grew up with stable systems around them and few distractions. Pre-internet era, most kids matured without knowing much about how other people lived. Kids knew about their family and friends but almost nothing about the lives of people in other social classes, religions or locations. Success was simply defined too. Get good grades, get a good job, find a partner, get a mortgage, have children and stay out of trouble. If you followed that formula you were generally considered accomplished. Along this path, your friends would stay close and you would only compare yourself to the hundred or so people in your social circle.

Today it's not as easy to raise kids who are sure to be successful and happy with their achievements. People change jobs every few years, industries morph constantly, opportunities cluster around huge cities and small towns might not have much to offer. Family homes can cost fifteen to twenty times the average wage. In your child's career they will mix with people from all over the world, they will encounter incredibly complex problems, they will be displaced, they will be isolated from their friendship groups at times and they will have to navigate this fast-changing landscape using their wits. Life is no longer simple and being successful has become difficult.

As today's children are increasingly familiar with the lives of celebrities and billionaires, it's easy for them to start believing that everyone has a jet, a Ferrari and multiple homes around the world without any understanding of how these trappings are achieved or how rarely they happen. Kids can compare themselves with their most talented, beautiful and lucky counterparts from anywhere on earth. Without any understanding of how to navigate this world or how to set and pursue worthy goals they can feel resentful, powerless and even depressed.

This new and complex world poses a challenge for parents. How do you prepare your kids for a world that is constantly changing? How do you prepare someone to be thrown into a melting pot of conflicting ideas, cultures, opportunities and expectations?

One thing is certain, the school system is not going to solve the problem for you. Schools will largely focus on the same subjects they always have. English, mathematics, art, geography, history, science, music, religion and the like still make up the bulk of what your child will learn at school.

Undoubtedly, some teachers are entrepreneurial. However, most have never started a business, let alone grown a successful company. Many went to university then straight back into the school system. This system faces its own set of issues but it is one of the few institutions that changes relatively slowly – a school today doesn't look massively different to a school twenty years ago.

We are probably some time away from schools teaching skills like negotiation, sales, marketing, finance, pitching, product creation or strategic joint venturing, but if they did, they would have an obvious problem to deal with: many of the skills that make you successful in life get you into trouble at school.

In business, it's considered smart to get someone else to do your complex homework. You may be rewarded for being disruptive and getting the attention of others. You have to be creative with your approach and should challenge authority and question the status quo rather than simply accepting what you are told.

Most schools generally frown upon these sorts of behaviours so it is your job as a parent to carefully introduce a set of skills that they won't teach your kids: entrepreneurial skills. They don't need to be running a business, employing people and presenting pitch decks to investors. Being a kid is stressful enough.

What we are suggesting is introducing your kids to entrepreneurial ideas. Share with them a unique perspective on the world of work, money, investment, income and opportunity through an entrepreneurial lens. Doing so will set them up better prepared for the world around them.

In this book you will see stories from hundreds of parents showing how they have done this. Many of the ideas are simple – like describing work as something fun, letting kids buy the groceries online, paying pocket money for key results rather than chores and getting a teen to pitch for that pet they want you to buy using PowerPoint slides. Simple ideas that are fun, entrepreneurial and valuable.

We have broken the book up into four key areas of raising entrepreneurial kids:

1.   Mindset

We will share stories from parents that can help you create a positive, confident, resourceful mindset in your children. This mindset will be based on a set of values that you create together and a tool to help them to have a life and future career on their own terms. A defining characteristic of entrepreneurship is freedom: freedom to make your own decisions on how you spend your time and who you spend it with. This section of the book will help you teach your child that not only is anything possible, but it's also all within their control.

Instilling them with beliefs and values that are aligned to entrepreneurship isn't just about doing business. This mindset will give them an awareness of opportunities to create something of value, to positively disrupt a situation, to collaborate towards an outcome or to make money on their own terms. Rather than seeing the world of work as something to be endured and tolerated, you'll give them an understanding that work can be fun, creative and rewarding.

2.   Skills

Once the entrepreneurial mindset is established, we move to sharing stories from parents and guardians who are developing the skills required to thrive as an entrepreneur. These include coming up with ideas, learning about how an industry works, developing systems, setting and reaching goals as well as selling, pitching, organising and working with others. You don't need a business or even a business idea to practise these skills; there are opportunities in everyday interactions between parents and children.

Giving them a chance to develop skills like sales, pitching, marketing, product creation, accounting, customer service, deal-making, negotiation and leadership will change their life no matter what they do for work. Rather than purely focusing on the academic skills that are needed to get good grades, raising entrepreneurial kids is about developing the skills that are often associated with dynamic careers.

3. Opportunities

We learn by doing. We also learn by experimenting, tinkering and making mistakes. In the opportunities section of this book we'll take you through how to make the most of your own work, the internet and your networks to get your kids involved and practise acting like an entrepreneur. You don't need friends in high places or loads of cash to create valuable learning opportunities; you just need to know how to identify them.

In this section you will see examples of parents and guardians who are providing children with a chance to express their new skills, earn some money, seize opportunities and put something creative into the world. Rather than shielding your children from the outside world, you'll learn new ways to protect them as they interact with real-life entrepreneurial scenarios that teach powerful lessons.

4. Mentoring

Entrepreneurs at any stage of business can benefit from the guidance of a coach or mentor. Coaching is based on the premise that the answers are there if you look for them. A coach or a mentor guides kids towards resourceful ideas and behaviours without necessarily telling them the answers. The purpose of this stage is to cultivate independence and self-reliance and develop your child's critical thinking skills to be able to choose their own path and make the best decisions accordingly. We talk you through how to be a solid mentor, including leading by example and asking questions that encourage and contextualise situations.

You may also encourage your children to meet and learn about entrepreneurs who create jobs rather than work in them, who have invented something, done deals or managed a successful business. Introducing your kids to entrepreneurial role models in the real world can leave a lasting impression and an 'if it's possible for them, it's possible for me' attitude.

In these four categories you'll see a range of age-appropriate ways to raise an entrepreneurial kid. Children as young as four will respond to some of the basic ideas like thinking big, helping others and being rewarded, and paying money for things. For those with teens, you'll see the spark of creativity ignite if you challenge them to earn money selling items online, offering a car cleaning service in the neighbourhood or helping a small business get set up with an Instagram account.

The entrepreneurial skills you develop in your child today might be the key to them having a great career, starting a game-changing business or solving a meaningful problem at scale.

In addition to this book, we have established an online community of parents and guardians who want to raise entrepreneurial kids. In this group you can share your experiences and results and learn from others as they experiment with this unique parenting style.

Ultimately, the bigger picture of raising an entrepreneurial kid is not about pushing your child to be the next Steve Jobs or Anita Roddick; it doesn't even matter if they never start a business. What matters most is that your child feels a sense of control as they grow and learn about the world: they feel they have the power to set goals that are right for them, pursue those goals and to pivot when they choose to. These ideas and skills will serve them no matter what they choose to do.

There is also a deeper message that might come through in some of the stories you read in this book. Although none of the parents, grandparents or entrepreneurs say it directly, there's a sense that we live in a time where the world needs good leaders. Raising a child with this set of skills might be the most important thing you could do for the world.

Entrepreneurship isn't about balance sheets and profit targets; it's about serving others in a scalable and sustainable way. It's about finding solutions to complex problems and enrolling others into your vision. As humanity moves closer to the edge of what's possible and what's wise, more than ever we need people who are ready to lead in a world that is increasingly faced with difficult decisions.

HOW TO USE THIS BOOK

JODIE

How To Raise Entrepreneurial Kids includes examples of what my parents taught me and what Daniel's parents taught him, as well as the experience of hundreds of other entrepreneurs, business leaders and parents. It also contains stories from the childhoods of well-known entrepreneurs.

This book is a framework, a toolkit and a force for social mobility. It can be used as a handbook, for ideas, guidance and conversation starters you can incorporate and experiment with. There will likely be some you want to try out straight away, and others that require planting the seed or setting up the right opportunity.

Within the four sections of this book there are several sub-sections, each presenting a different way of raising entrepreneurial kids, coupled with examples and ideas to try. For some of the most effective, the ideas presented are simple but are not to be overlooked in their potential for someone's future. Fostering the environment in which entrepreneurial kids can develop isn't immediate. It involves subtle and consistent messaging, so think of this more like a marathon than a sprint.

The mindset and mentoring sections can be applied to children of all ages – the younger the better. How someone sees themselves, their ability and potential, can be shaped even with simple phrases and coaching techniques. The skills and opportunities sections work to build upon these foundations.

You can decide the appropriateness of each idea for your kids. Ability and understanding differ wildly even within age groups. What resonates with one eight-year-old might not with another. If you find an example your family isn't ready for, make a note to revisit it in the future. You may find that different points are relevant at different ages or life stages. Apply the more advanced techniques as your kids grow up and are ready to be introduced to them.

You might not see instant feedback of the methods in the book working. You might, however, see signs that someone is starting to forge their own path by asking questions and starting to problem solve. You might spot a shift from a fixed to growth mindset. You might notice an increase in confidence, creativity or independence or sparks of enthusiasm. You might notice fewer tantrums and more lightbulb moments. The changes might be subtle, and you might only notice them in specific situations such as when someone is challenged or put on the spot.

These are the traits that mean, regardless of their past, someone is becoming far better equipped for a happy and successful future. A future where they can make it happen, where 'it' is anything they want.

PART 1
ENTREPRENEURIAL MINDSET

DANIEL

There's not a lot of silence when you have three kids under the age of six. It often means you need to check in to see that the television isn't about to be covered in crayon colours or someone isn't about to toboggan down the stairs on a sibling.

Inevitably, the silence is broken with an upset screech resulting from someone's creation being messed with – a tower knocked down, a piece of art vandalised or a catastrophic model-train derailment.

One particular day my quiet cup of tea was interrupted with, 'Ethan knocked over my Lego tower!' As I went to inspect the rubble, I said to my five-year-old, 'You know, the fun part about Lego is building it? When it gets knocked over you get to have even more fun doing more building.' On this occasion he smiled and agreed – he understood that the fun part was building it, not having it.

This simple idea is powerful. Disruption happens to us throughout our lives. Almost every ten years there is some sort of social or economic disruption that catches everyone off guard – a recession, a pandemic, a natural disaster, a seismic technological shift or a huge political swing. Add to that the stuff that happens in our personal lives that upends our best laid plans – a sick relative, moving cities for work, a death in the family, a career change or business failure, a divorce or an injury.

I have met with adults who are still stuck on something that happened to them a decade or two ago. I once met someone who was visibly shaken and paralysed with fear as he talked about a terrible personal event that was preventing him from starting a business. He told me how things were going well for him but then his father got sick, his wife left him and his business failed all within a year. We were discussing the situation for at least ten minutes before I discovered that this had happened twelve years earlier.

Conversely, I know a man who got sick one weekend, went into hospital, became unconscious and woke up to discover all of his limbs had been amputated to prevent meningitis from killing him. In the months that followed, he committed himself to the idea that it would be the greatest thing that ever happened to him. He went on to write a book, start a business, travel the world and get engaged to a phenomenal woman. He cheekily said to me, 'I was on track to work in the same boring job all of my brothers do. Now I travel the world having incredible adventures – they'd probably give their arms and legs to live the way I do.'

Life is full of unexpected events that topple our hopes and dreams and we should realistically expect the unexpected to cause havoc every few years. The mindset that 'the fun part is building it, not having it' is something that adults could probably benefit from as well as kids.

As a parent or guardian of a young person, you have the power to instil a mindset that will serve them for life. You can teach your kids that they are victims or you can teach them that they are largely in control. You can teach them that they are stuck with their lot in life or that they are free to change their circumstances in most cases. You can teach them that the world is a scarce place full of turmoil and despair or that the world is abundant and full of triumph and change.

The way they see the world will depend upon their mindset. Entrepreneurs have a unique mindset. They tend to see problems as opportunities, they see complexity and challenge as a 'barrier to entry' that protects them and they view resources as a factor of resourcefulness. More than most, they see that they can change things if they want to. They aren't fixed in the belief that the world simply is the way it is; they are open to the idea that the world can be made better.

As you'll see in this section of the book, there are many ways to strengthen the attitudes and beliefs that will serve your kids most. Deliberately shaping a kid's mindset towards empowerment, optimism, resilience and courage will pay off in the long term and even in the here and now. You'll read about parents who reframe failure for their kids, who use little mantras and maxims to reinforce useful ideas and who help their kids to dream big and go for it.

Several weeks after teaching my son that the fun part is 'building something, not having something', I witnessed a wonderful interaction. He was immersed in an imaginary world, setting up his train set when his brother steamrolled through it, sending all the carefully placed pieces scattering. Without prompting, he smiled at his brother and said, 'Thank you, now we can build it all over again. Do you want to help me?' His brother readily agreed and the two of them set to work. That tiny mindset shift had made all the difference – rather than throwing a tantrum, he got straight back on track doing what he loved. If he keeps that mindset, he will get a lot more out of life.

FAMILY ALIGNMENT

DANIEL

Conventional wisdom suggests that when a child asks for something, you must never change your mind or deviate from your original answer or else the child will learn that they can negotiate with you. Would it be so bad if your child felt confident in their ability to impact a decision they didn't like? Separate from the understandable desire you might have to lay down the law in the short term, it is worth considering that some of the most successful entrepreneurs on the planet are powerful negotiators.

Unlike most adults, great entrepreneurs are confident that they can improve their arguments and change outcomes they don't like. To help negotiation skills with children, a different approach can be to tell them that if they talk nicely, improve their argument and choose the right time to put forward their case, it is entirely possible to get a different response than the initial rejection they receive. This is a more empowered mindset to instil.

While failure is often viewed negatively, entrepreneurs have an interesting relationship with it. In most cases they view failure as an essential part of success and not something that is permanent or lasting. Entrepreneurs want to fail fast so they can learn and pivot.

For example, learning to ride a bike without stabilisers isn't just an opportunity to develop cycling skills, it can also be an opportunity to instil a powerful mindset that can be applied to many scenarios. 'Mistakes are part of learning' and 'every winner was once a beginner' are simple phrases young kids can apply to riding a bike that will still be in the recesses of their minds as young adults.

As a parent or guardian, you get to choose what gets celebrated in the lives of your children. You probably buy a cake for celebrating a birthday and you probably proudly display trophies and ribbons collected at sporting days. It's possible to also embrace failure as well. Not just with a trite 'at least you tried' or a trophy for participation – kids need to know that it's important to win – but with a dinner table conversation which acknowledges that failing at something is always an important step towards triumph.

Developing a vision, mission and values for your family is a powerful way to shape the mindset of your kids. If I told you that my business has a written vision and a mission and values statement you probably wouldn't be surprised because most fast-growth companies have put thought into this to shape the behaviour, attitudes and culture of their organisations. Why then would it be strange to put thought into this sort of document for your family? In fact, many of the world's most successful families do discuss their family values, vision and mission and many document it. Knowing what is expected of them can have a profound impact on the mindset of your kids.

ACTIONABLES

- Have some fun creating your family's mission statement. It might include your family rules, how you talk to and treat each other and what you like to do together.
- Encourage conversation about what goes into your mission statement.
- You could even display it somewhere prominent, so it's always in view.

When my husband Kelin and I got married, I created what I call a family playbook. As a business owner, I have a vision and a strategy for my business, so why wouldn't I have one for my family too? The playbook contains our values and what we stand for, including what we most passionately believe in, so that we can pass that onto our children in a really intentional way. The playbook includes fun things we fill out together like 'our family mission', 'top five family values to live by', 'reasons why Carrie thinks Kelin is amazing' and vice-versa, and 'how to make Carrie/Kelin feel special!' I think it's about getting intentional about who you are and what you stand for, to create a strong foundation from which to achieve extraordinary things.

Carrie Green, Female Entrepreneur Association

I learned that it was fine to try and to fail, that I would regret the things I didn't do more than the ones that I did, and to honor all forms of work. They taught me to treasure our freedom and to make the most of my short time here. My mother was incredibly gifted in sales and my father was comfortable talking with the janitor or royalty. Through them, I learned that making someone else feel welcomed, safe and good about themselves is the essence of the hospitality business. We strive to hit that mark every day at our ventures.

Spencer Clements, William Cole Companies

My parents raised two daughters who are now both entrepreneurs. They were liberal, feminist, left-leaning, social-conscious residents of Berkeley, California. They raised my sister and me with POW bracelets and my mom was 'Another Mother for Peace'. She even had an afro and wore flowing Peter Max-style clothing. Throughout my childhood, my parents repeatedly told us, 'You can do anything and be anything.' They never assumed what we would be and who we would become and encouraged us to explore the world.

Lora Poepping, Plum Coaching & Consulting

LARRY ELLISON

Known for: Co-founder of Oracle

What else: The sixth wealthiest person in the world, Larry has signed 'The Giving Pledge', committing at least half of his fortune to philanthropic causes.

Ellison has never known his biological father and met his biological mother only once. He says his adoptive family (his biological mother's sister, Lilian Spellman Ellison and her husband Louis Ellison), Jewish immigrants from Europe, took the name 'Ellison' after Ellis Island. He grew up working class in an apartment building in Chicago.

Within Ellison's family, his mother was kind, caring and loving. His father, however, was strict, stubborn and exacting, an accountant who was forever telling Ellison that he was a good-for-nothing. Despite this, Ellison grew up independent, self-assured and uncompromising, which led to constant quarrels and misunderstandings with his father as well as with his peers.

At school, Ellison was interested in complicated subjects such as spaceship construction, technology and engineering. He was a mediocre student and played squash, volleyball and hockey. Ellison was considered smart but bridled under authority. He attended the University of Illinois and the University of Chicago, quit both and headed west to work for technology companies.

In his oral history, he recalled, 'I never took a computer science class in my life. I got a job working as a programmer; I was largely self-taught. I just picked up a book and started programming.'[1]

Ellison named his first product 'Oracle Version 2', despite it being version one. He and his co-founders thought that no customer would want to take a risk on a brand new product.[2]

FINANCIAL MODELS

JODIE

Whether intentionally or not, your family operates a certain financial model of how it views, earns, saves and spends money. This will be the default financial model of your children, effective from when they start to manage their own money.

There are as many different models of financial management as there are people. While Robert Kiyosaki's bestselling book, *Rich Dad Poor Dad*, tells you that building a property portfolio to create passive income is the way to go,[3] a careers advisor suggests climbing the corporate ladder so your six-figure salary can pay for the house, car and holiday of your dreams. A money-saving magazine might discuss clipping coupons for your groceries and the benefits of individual savings accounts (ISAs) while an independent financial advisor suggests you buy a commercial property for your pension fund and a digital nomad tells you to secure contracts that cover your flights and Airbnbs so you can see the world. Suddenly, the assumptions we have been making (and teaching) for years come into question. Is it right to get a mortgage? Is it right to save? Who is right? Is anyone right? Which concepts should we introduce to our children?

To complicate this further, a third of millennials will never own their own home,[4] personal debt continues to rise[5] and the social pressure to consume has never been so intertwined in the fabric of our existence. Many of the role models children have are YouTube vloggers or Instagram influencers. The old system of 'salary in, expenses out' doesn't match up to the reality we now face, and certainly not the reality today's children will face.

An individual's attitude towards money is equally, if not more, important than understanding the pounds and pence of it all. What any individual is comfortable with is largely dependent on their upbringing, current situation and future aspirations, as well as their role models.

Financial understanding will differ wildly between generations. Concepts such as property crashes, cryptocurrency and angel investing, to name a few, mean that each generation's experience of how (or how not) to make and spend money comes from a different foundation. Compare the baby boomers of today with the eight-year-old children in school. The huge growth of the gig economy and the prevalence of freelancing as an occupation will mean that these kids will more than likely never be paid the same amount at the same time each month. They might never experience a salary.

Consider these questions:

- Is dispensing monthly pocket money conditioning children to expect a salary? Is this out-dated?

- What are the pros and cons of earning a steady salary? What are the pros and cons of contract work?

- How is money being made? What is someone buying – your time, knowledge or a product?

- How helpful are phrases often thrown around, such as 'money doesn't grow on trees' or 'we'll never be able to afford that'?

ACTIONABLES

- How often is making money as a kid linked to doing chores, and are there other ways?

- How can we instil a belief in financial abundance and help kids view money as something that can be made by many methods?

- Notice when you are defining money or having money as something unattainable, or sharing limiting beliefs.

I encourage my daughter Isabel to be entrepreneurial by giving her an allowance. This encourages her to live on a budget and buy only what she can afford. Isabel helps with the ordering and testing of products sold on my store. She helps prepare and package products for shipment. She is in the process of testing slime recipes to start her own Etsy store.

Deborah Rogers, The Gifted Rat

When it comes to my own children, I encourage their entrepreneurial spirit by... not giving them any money! If my kids, now ages nineteen, fifteen and eleven want something, they have to earn it. But first, they have to figure out how they can earn it.

Alina Adams, NYC School Secrets podcast

Growing up, I know my parents always wanted to be able to buy us the things our friends had but they really couldn't. They even tell us that today. We lived in rural Alabama so there weren't many jobs to be had as a kid. I found that if I wanted spending money, I would have to earn it. I did this mowing grass and pulling weeds in peanut fields while I was too young to drive to a job. Once I was able to drive, I was able to take better jobs for higher pay. Allowing me to pursue income opportunities on my own as a kid was a driving force to me wanting to be an entrepreneur.

Doug Mitchell, Ogletree Financial

ESTHER AFUA OCLOO

Known for: One of the founders of Women's World Banking

What else: A pioneer in the practice of micro-lending in her home country of Ghana, Esther won an award from The Hunger Project to 'outstanding leaders from every level and every sector of society' who have impacted over ten million lives.

Born into a poverty-stricken family, Ocloo realised the significance of being economically independent early in life. Her desire to focus on empowering women came from her desire for others not to suffer the austerity she saw around her growing up.

When Ocloo graduated from high school, she was gifted ten shillings (about a dollar) from her aunt. She used the money to buy oranges, sugar and other ingredients necessary to make a dozen jars of marmalade. She wanted to make some marmalade that could be sold for a profit.

In an interview Ocloo said, 'I was determined to turn that ten shillings into two pounds at least. With six shillings, I bought the ingredients to make marmalade and went to the street side to sell the jars of marmalade. Within an hour, I had sold all my jars and turned six shillings into twelve! I was so excited, I treated myself to a delicious lunch.'[6] Ocloo had teachers who believed in her. They asked her to supply the school with her marmalade twice a week, thus becoming her first regular client, because they were impressed with the quality as well as her conviction.

DREAMING BIG

JODIE

There's a phrase often attributed to Aristotle, but actually from the American philosopher Will Durant: 'We are what we repeatedly do.'[7] Another way of thinking about this is that we can't be the noun without doing the verb. To be a writer, we must write. To be a singer, we must sing. There's no way of being a ballerina without going to ballet practice, and it's the same with any sport or musical instrument. Growing up, I remember learning the clear distinction between *saying* you wanted to be good at something and *practising* to be good at something. If I said I wanted to do something and had committed, I was held to it; no amount of kicking or screaming would allow me to not show up.

As all entrepreneurs know, it's not enough to write down your goals and then wait for them to happen; you have to be deliberate about achieving them and put steps in place to get closer each day.

In practice, this could start with family discussions about the future and dreaming big about what it could hold. It could involve looking at professional sportspeople or industry experts and talking about how they reached their level. You can't just win Wimbledon, you have to practise playing tennis every day, do your stretches, win matches and keep fit. A family friend called Freddie, age five, said he wanted to be a fireman when he grows up. 'Of course you can be a fireman,' his mum replied. 'Now tell me all the things you'll need to learn.' The purpose wasn't to put Freddie off wanting to be a fireman, it was to get him thinking about everything that it involves, including the hard work in training, passing the tests and sliding down the pole.

Entrepreneur Chris Myers has written about growing up with the 40% rule, made popular by Jesse Itzler in his book *Living with a SEAL: 31 days training with the toughest man on the planet*. Myers explains: 'The 40% rule is simple: When your mind is telling you that you're done, that you're exhausted, that you cannot possibly go any further, you're only actually 40% done.'[8] Growing up, Myers was always told, 'If it's too hard for someone else, it's just right for us.' He calls it a phrase that he both loved and hated. I love the idea that he was taught to approach things that might, on the surface, seem too difficult. What a great way to encourage someone to strive to achieve, and to not be afraid of hard work.

ACTIONABLES

- Paint a picture of what an extraordinary life would look like. In this life, where would you go? Who would you meet? What would you wear?

- Set some goals. Talk about what you could achieve in the next week, year or five years.

- Scale the goals up. How could you achieve twice that? What about ten times as much as that?

- Look at the lives and careers of people you read about and see in the news. Talk about what they do and how they got there.

'Be better today than yesterday.' This was a piece of advice my father gave me when I was in high school, and he wasn't at all speaking about business. He often saw me dreaming big dreams (and he encouraged the dreaming), but then one day told me this piece of advice. Just be better today than you were yesterday, and you'll get there. I've adopted this 100% into start-up life.

John Tabis, The Bouqs Company

I was taught that I could be anything and do anything. I was taught to politely question everything and not to necessarily take no for an answer. I come from a very working-class family and I have always wanted to be a lawyer. People from where I was from always said to me that I would never do it and people like us didn't become lawyers or go to university. My mum refused to take no for an answer and eventually got me a scholarship at a good school and taught me that if I worked hard enough, I could do and achieve anything. My gran taught me that what other people think of me is none of my business and to be kind and to treat others fairly and with respect. My mum and my gran's unfailing belief in me meant that I ignored the nay-sayers and strived for what I wanted. I'm now the youngest partner at the world's largest listed law firm

Naomi Pryde, DWF LLP

While I don't have any children of my own, I do have some influence on my nieces and nephews. I present the example of someone that has control over their time and location. Most adults in their life have regular jobs that dictate what they do, when and where. I try to ask them questions about what they want and how they can leverage their skills, knowledge and opportunities to achieve those goals.

Frank Jones, OptSus Marketing

CARRIE GREEN

Known for: Founder of the Female Entrepreneur Association

What else: Has over 600,000 female entrepreneurs in her network and wrote the bestselling book, *She Means Business*.

Before Green was ten years old, her business owner dad sent her, along with her three siblings, on a course that helped her learn about visualisation and the power of the mind. On this course, she learned how to create a mind palace and access it when she needed answers to questions, how to wash away negativity and how to visualise the future she wanted to create for herself. Her dad also showed her Jim Rohn videos about creating successful habits and proceeded to do impressions of Jim around the house, just for fun.

Despite Green picking up skills and attitudes that were securing her future, she was placed in the bottom sets at school and her teachers thought she had learning difficulties. Green admits she played up to being thought of as a naughty kid, being silly and joking around in lessons.

Green's dad taught her techniques for avoiding negativity from the words or actions of others. One technique was to imagine you have a giant bell jar that you can place over yourself to deflect negativity from anyone else and ensure it won't affect you. Green took all of this teaching on board, perhaps to prove herself to the educators who had overlooked her, and she made her own goal folder in which she included printouts and descriptions of what she wanted her life to look, feel and even smell like. The goal folder includes a photoshopped print-screen of a bank statement where she has £136,000,000 in the bank.[9]

INDEPENDENCE

JODIE

Metaphorically throw someone in at the deep end and they either sink or swim. The entrepreneurs we heard from were regularly thrown in at the deep end, but they were consistently reassured that they would figure out how to prosper. Their parents became their biggest champions, giving them the confidence and belief required.

Once these children had a taste of independence, they searched for it everywhere. They started to make their own decisions, welcomed the chance to take ownership of a process, and fiercely protected their solo pursuits.

The opportunities for independence started small then were built up when appropriate for the individual. Choosing outfits, booking appointments and planning their weekend led to independently thinking of solutions to problems or creative ideas. Each stage developed ownership, responsibility and a desire for someone to push themselves – vital skills for entrepreneurs.

One of my biggest bugbears today is being presented with a problem by someone who hasn't thought about any potential solutions. When this happens, as a parent or manager, it's easy to go into problem-solving mode and start suggesting the solutions yourself or to say, 'I'll take care of it,' without further discussion.

This doesn't help. It only develops dependency on someone else to think about the problem and find the potential solutions. It outsources the thinking to another person and trains the problem-solver to rely on others. It trains helplessness, which is definitely not a trait common in entrepreneurs, at least not the good ones.

A longer-term strategy, requiring more patience in the short term, is to teach someone else to own the problem and be responsible for solving it. The simplest way to do this is to respond by asking questions. Keep asking questions until the solution is reached, then highlight and reassure them that they had the solution all along.

I FOUND THIS 'GANDALF STICK'
AND KIDS PAY 10¢ TO MAKE A WISH

ACTIONABLES

Develop a problem-solving mindset by using these phrases when presented with a problem:

- What could have caused this problem?
- Can you think of five ways this could be fixed?
- What have you tried so far? Why didn't that work?
- Has this problem happened before? If so, how did you solve it then?
- What would you do if I wasn't here? What would you do next?

For each of these questions, the answer might not come straight away. Resist the urge to fill the silence. Get comfortable in the gap between the question and the answer, because that's where the best thinking happens. Give helpful prompts and add reassurance that they can come to the answer, but avoid taking over completely.

Level one is your child reaching the solution from your questioning. Level two is them being able to ask and answer the questions without your input. Given time, responses will change, for example: 'Mum, the TV remote is broken, fix it,' can develop into 'Mum, I noticed the TV remote isn't working. I suspected it might be the batteries so I've taken some out of the smoke alarm to test my theory and now the remote is working. So, I've solved the problem and can watch my TV show but now I need to go to the shop to buy some more batteries for the smoke alarm.'

Since my daughter is only two, there's not much interest in discussions around pricing strategies, tax planning, HR processes, etc. However, what both my wife and I try to do is encourage her as much as possible to be independent and do things for herself. This includes anything from chores (she loves helping us wipe tables) to getting dressed to picking an activity at the park. What most entrepreneurs want above all else is freedom and independence, so I hope encouraging this mindset from a young age will give her the confidence to blaze her own trail sometime long from now.

Ian Wright, Merchant Machine

Because 'they never had anything' my Cuban parents never fixed anything we broke. This forced my hot-tempered and highly competitive siblings and me to be resourceful and inventive. I recall breaking a Nintendo controller and using popsicle sticks and duct tape to fix it. It actually worked better!

Laz Versalles, Accesa Labs

Being the child of immigrants, my entrepreneurial drive was actually shaped by what my parents could not do. Because they were busy surviving and adjusting to life in America, I was often left on my own – to discover my own interests, motivate myself and be independent at a very early age. That self-drive serves me very well today, especially in a business environment that is in constant flux.

Quynh Mai, MI&C

DAYMOND JOHN

Known for: Founder of FUBU

What else: In 2009 he became one of the original celebrity investors on the USA TV show *Shark Tank.*

Growing up in Queens, Daymond John's mother taught him that he was in charge of his own destiny. She told him that he had to work hard for everything that he wanted out of life. John learned the power of sales in first grade, where he would scrape the paint off pencils and paint his customer's name on them for a fee. At the same time, he was shovelling snow in the winter and raking leaves in the fall.

At age ten, his parents divorced and from that point on he was raised by his mum. After the divorce, John became the man of the house, tasked with helping to support it. One early job entailed handing out flyers for $2 an hour. He was also an apprentice electrician and used to wire abandoned buildings in the Bronx. His mum said to him, 'Listen, you're going to have to figure out what you're doing the rest of your life, one way or another.'[10]

In a media interview, John explained, 'Then all of a sudden there was this amazing music. It came out of the Bronx and it made its way into Queens. It was called hip-hop...There was this guy in Queens and he was becoming really well-known and he was making a living selling this music and I didn't realise that you could make a living doing something you love...'[11] John's incredible work ethic, combined with the realisation that you could make a living doing what you love, made him unstoppable.

CONFIDENCE

JODIE

Entrepreneurs are confident people. It doesn't mean they're loud or they monopolise conversations. It means they are sure of who they are and what they stand for. They are confident in their own ability to do something.

Like many entrepreneurs, I don't mind getting up on stage or being put on the spot and will pretty much chat to anyone. Growing up I assumed everyone else was the same. It wasn't until I had left school that I realised that stress, anxiety and nerves were experiences that could affect someone's ability to do what they wanted to do. It seemed crazy that these things could hold someone back, having never considered them as real concepts before.

Dissecting the reasons behind why some people are affected by nerves and why some people seem ever-confident gives three points to explore further:

1. Labelling

There are two derivations of the word 'stress'. The first and the most commonly used is from 'distress', defined as extreme anxiety, sorrow or pain. The second, coined by Hans Selye in 1975, is 'eustress'. Literally, the 'good stress' – this pressure is associated with positive feelings and health benefits.[12]

Of course, being in a genuine 'fight or flight' scenario – chased by bears or confronted at knifepoint – is different, but in an everyday situation, chances are the physical symptoms are a good thing.

Most people will have experienced an unsettled feeling in their tummy before a talk, before being on camera or doing anything with an audience including sport, but what if it's framed as an adrenaline rush rather than anxiety or nerves? Labelling that feeling you get before you go on stage with negative terminology might mean you shy away from it rather than work on being a great public speaker, for example. If I'm about to do something that is making my heart rate increase and making me feel a bit jittery, I see that as a good thing. I think of the adrenaline as being on my side, as helping me perform at my best. This could also be called eustress.

2. Channelling the confidence of others

There was a girl in my primary school class who was always so confident. I remember being in awe of how she could always say what she thought, she could dance around the playground like no one was watching and she loved taking the lead in school plays or putting her hand up in class to answer a question. At the time, perhaps subconsciously, I channelled her behaviour and mirrored her confidence when I felt like I needed to.

I was defining the person I wanted to be and then taking the steps to become that person. Soon this became a habit and I didn't need to channel the behaviour of my friend, I just became a more confident person. Now I use the phrase, 'How would the person I want to be do the things I'm about to do?'

3. Framing a situation

If something is framed as a really big, scary deal, chances are it will be treated like one. If something is framed as something really positive, exciting and enjoyable, it will be treated differently. When I was younger, my parents were keen to offer support but treated me as if I was perfectly capable. I recall phrases like, 'Why wouldn't you be able to?', 'what's the worst that could happen?' and 'how hard can it be?' being used. They weren't being dismissive, they were helping me find

29

the perspective I needed to maintain confidence. It helped me realise that the overthinking I might have been doing was unfounded, and that reframing the task and preparing for it would be the best way of making a success of any potentially daunting situation.

ACTIONABLES

Confidence is essential to entrepreneurship and raising confident young people is possible. In practice this might mean:

- Playing down the scariness of events like school plays, recitals or exams.

- Being careful not to label upcoming experiences negatively.

- Explaining that pre-performance jitters are a good thing.

- Working from the assumption that someone is perfectly capable but offering support.

- Noticing the confident traits in other people and discussing how to emulate them.

My parents have been the key to my success. I don't remember ever disappointing them or failing as a child. They consistently built me up and emotionally spoiled me. I could do no wrong. Because of them, I've always had a lot of confidence and support, providing me with the foundation to never have fear. If I ever did fail, I would pick myself up and move forward having learned from those lessons.

Bryanne Lawless-DeGoede, BLND Public Relations

Somewhat cliché, yet profound, when your parents tell you from a young age that 'you can do anything you set your mind to.' I believed them, and believed in myself as a result of their words and support. As a little girl, I was determined, focused and driven to reach my goals. I was going to sell the most candy bars, magazines, or girl scout cookies during school or activity fundraisers. I would set a goal and achieve it.

Romy Taormina, Psi Bands

My stepdad instilled in me a love for education, a deep sense of discipline and commitment to the pursuit of excellence. He helped teach me the importance of confidence. When I would tell him an answer to a question, his response was always, 'Are you sure?' After I expressed my assurance the first time, he would nudge again and make sure, 'Are you absolutely sure that's right?' When I would waiver after that second prompt, he would offer, 'You were right. Don't doubt yourself.' I think about this a lot now as a female CEO in the competitive tech industry. Confidence is key and decisiveness is critical.

Autumn Manning, YouEarnedIt

CHRIS GARDNER

Known for: Founder of Gardner, Rich & Co

What else: His story was turned into the movie, *The Pursuit of Happyness*.

Gardner says that, 'Without knowing the names, circumstances, or social conditions I consciously chose to break every cycle that I was born into. Child abandonment, child abuse, alcoholism, domestic violence, fear, poverty and illiteracy.'[13]

During the late 1960s, Gardner was influenced by political figures like Eldridge Cleaver, Martin Luther King and Malcolm X. According to Gardner, his mother encouraged him to believe in himself and sowed the seeds of self-reliance. Gardner quotes her as saying, 'You can only depend on yourself. The cavalry ain't coming.'[14]

Gardner did not have many positive male role models as a child. While in foster care, Gardner first became acquainted with his three maternal uncles: Archibald, Willie and Henry. Of the three, Henry had the most profound influence on him, entering Gardner's world at a time when he most needed a positive father figure.

Gardner remembers a defining moment when he was sixteen and watching a college basketball game on TV. When he commented that one of the players would make a million dollars, 'My mum said, "Son, one day it will be you who'll make a million dollars." Until she said those words the thought had never entered my mind.' He absorbed her words, which stuck with him through the decades that followed.[15]

ADAPTABILITY

JODIE

You might be familiar with IQ (intelligence quotient) and EQ (emotional quotient, or emotional intelligence), but let me introduce AQ: adaptability quotient. This is loosely defined as 'the ability to pivot and flourish in an environment of fast and frequent change'.[16]

'IQ is the minimum you need to get a job, but AQ is how you will be successful over time,' says Natalie Fratto, a New York-based vice-president at Goldman Sachs who became interested in AQ when she was investing in tech start-ups. She has subsequently presented a popular TED talk on the subject.[17]

Fratto says AQ is not just the capacity to absorb new information, but the ability to work out what is relevant, unlearn obsolete knowledge, overcome challenges and to make a conscious effort to change. AQ involves flexibility, curiosity, courage, resilience and problem-solving skills. Sounds useful for a future entrepreneur, right?

When I was growing up, I would often be sitting on the sofa only to hear, 'Get ready, we're going out,' and to leave the house to go for a walk or to someone's house or to a shop. Regularly changing our family routine was just a part of growing up. Now I realise that it helped me learn to adapt quickly to new plans or new information. Even today, I don't freak out when something changes last minute or doesn't go to plan. I'm always in the mindset of 'OK, what can I do now?' and I'm sure it stems from change being welcomed from a young age.

The term for this is *routine flexibility*. That there might be a routine or plan in place, a best-case scenario, but if the restaurant runs out of your favourite meal or it starts to snow or there's a change of heart, it's not the end of the world and something else can be worked out. No biggie.

In a 2017 academic paper titled 'An investigation Into the Microdynamics of Routine Flexibility', two academics wrote about the benefits of routine flexibility to the survival of businesses in changing economic times, and the effect that someone's personal routine flexibility has on their being able to lose weight or make health improvements.[18] It makes perfect sense if you think about it.

AQ and routine flexibility are both about having a plan but also being happy for it to change. Making it no big deal if it does change. In the future, this means that if an opportunity comes up, it can be seized. Perhaps the plan is to complete school and go to university but a better opportunity might come up ahead of enrolling that an adaptable person can make the most of. Especially in a world where new technology or a global pandemic can open new opportunities at any moment, instilling nimbleness can keep options open.

ACTIONABLES

- Plan a detour or change of plan ahead of schedule but don't communicate it to your family. See how they react to a change of plan and assess why they coped well or badly with the news.

- Look for opportunities to practise adapting when everyday occurrences happen. Perhaps the washing hasn't dried and their favourite sweater isn't available, or the supermarket has run out of a key ingredient for dinner.

- Be open to last-minute bookings or plans and go along with them.

- Practise 'If this, then that' scenarios to be prepared for unexpected changes. For example: 'If you don't do your homework now, what will happen if you wake up late tomorrow?'

- Practise playing down the seriousness of change. Look for the good things. Ask, 'What's good about this?'

I was raised in a diverse household. We moved around a lot, generally every year or so, mainly between California and Arkansas. My mother was a single mother who worked a lot, so I played a big role in helping to raise my three sisters. At an early age, I learned how to quickly size up a situation, figure things out and problem solve. Being able to adapt to changing environments and situations has helped me get very good at looking at risks or problems as an opportunity to move forward and achieve more.

Autumn Manning, YouEarnedIt

As a military kid, we moved every few years and I learned how to start somewhere new while building a strong base within my family. Facing a new school, new friends and new activities, I gained resiliency and self-confidence. I'm glad my parents taught me to see change as an opportunity and practical skills to navigate new places.

Elizabeth Malson, Amslee Institute

My father worked in the regional newspaper industry, and as his career progressed our family found ourselves moving around the country from paper to paper, with the consequence that I found myself getting used to moving school and being the 'new boy' on a pretty regular basis. By the time I was thirteen I was starting my sixth school, including my third in that particular year, and while the moves were difficult and not without tears as good friends were left behind, looking back the experience definitely instilled in me an acceptance and comfort with change, and the ability to adapt and to quickly get used to new environments and people. Sport was certainly one 'device' I used to settle into a new school, be that playing or just talking about it. Sport is a great leveller, and team sports in particular are a great way to quickly establish new relationships and friendships, and a mix of football, rugby and cricket were constants that helped me to adapt swiftly as much else changed around me.

Paul Faulkner, Greater Birmingham Chambers of Commerce

ELON MUSK

Known for: CEO of SpaceX and Tesla

What else: In 2020, Musk and SpaceX made history when the company launched its Falcon 9 rocket into space, marking the first time a private company had sent a spacecraft containing humans to the International Space Station.

During his childhood in South Africa, Musk was an avid reader. His childhood reading included Isaac Asimov's *Foundation* series, from which he drew the lesson that 'you should try to take the set of actions that are likely to prolong civilisation, minimise the probability of a dark age and reduce the length of a dark age if there is one'.[19]

At about the time of his parent's divorce, when he was ten, Musk developed an interest in computers. He was often lost in daydreams about inventions and he taught himself how to program. When he was twelve, he sold his first software: a game he created called Blastar for $500. Musk was severely bullied throughout his childhood and was once hospitalised after a group of boys threw him down a flight of stairs. After that, he learned how to defend himself with karate and wrestling.

Although Musk's father insisted that Elon go to college in Pretoria, he was determined to move to the United States, saying, 'I remember thinking and seeing that America is where great things are possible, more than any other country in the world.'[20] Musk knew it would be easier to get to the United States from Canada and moved there against his father's wishes in June 1989, just before his eighteenth birthday, after obtaining a Canadian passport through his Canadian-born mother.

WHAT IS 'NORMAL'?

JODIE

There's a quote by Dr Seuss, that I love: 'I am what I am! That's a great thing to be!'[21] Another quote I love is, 'Whenever you find yourself on the side of the majority, it is time to pause and reflect' by Mark Twain.[22]

I remember the word 'normal' being kind of taboo in our house. Whenever my sister or I whined, 'Why can't you just be normal?' to our parents after they'd done something we considered embarrassing, the immediate response would be, 'What's normal?' perhaps followed by, 'Normal is boring!' I'm certain it stopped us striving to be normal and doing anything we could to fit in. Fitting in wasn't something that was positioned as being aspirational. It was aspirational to be remarkable.

We were never coerced into doing the same thing as any-one else and now I can see the advantages that had. Want to pursue a different interest? Order something different from the menu? Sure. Want to wear an outfit you're comfortable in instead of one you wear just for show? No problem. Want to hang out on your own and read a book? Start a business when everyone around you is getting a job? Go ahead.

At first, these types of responses may lead to crazy outfits and questionable decisions, but in the future they may lead to them confidently doing something differently, taking risks, not buckling to peer pressure or following a path because everyone else is.

Between siblings, families, cities, cultures and countries, what constitutes 'normal' will differ wildly. Everyone's version is different, so your family's can be too. There's no point trying to fit in with any single group, media representation or cultural norm because it only ends up closing minds, limiting possibilities and hindering progression and happiness.

Imagine a statement like, 'You can only have a successful business by being ruthless and mean.' Someone saying this might believe it to be true, but that's only based on their experience. It's the same with 'normal'; it's subjective. Someone else's version doesn't have to be yours.

ACTIONABLES

- Champion your child's choices or aspirations, even if they're not the popular choices, as well as any time they've demonstrated they've been happy to think and act for themselves.

- Don't chastise people you don't know for their choices. Someone wearing a crazy outfit or acting rather eccentric? Turn the comment into 'good for them' rather than one that belittles or criticises. Better still, don't comment at all.

- Practise acceptance of all differences and focus on difference as being a really good thing, as something that is needed to make the world an interesting place.

- Introduce them to people from different backgrounds to hear others' versions of 'normal' and how wildly different it can be across cultures and families.

- Celebrate differences by discussing the alternative. Imagine a world where everyone was exactly the same, and how boring it would be.

- Practise noticing the difference between something that is 100% true and something that someone believes to be 100% true.

Growing up in New York City's Greenwich Village during the 1970s, my parents taught me to be three things: creative, unique and self-motivated. My father was an actor and my mother a photographer, which meant the bar for creativity was incredibly high, but it also positioned me to think about the world in a unique way. That being said, our lifestyle was very different, which I came to realize more and more as I got older. My parents wanted me to see my creativity as my identifier, my uniqueness. One of the most effective ways my mother taught me to be creative and unique was insisting that I not only dressed myself but that I always picked out what I was going to wear every single day, even when that meant wearing a combo of corduroy pants with PRO-Keds, a *Star Wars* T-shirt and a pin-striped blazer to school. In my opinion, creativity, uniqueness and self-motivation are all necessary of an entrepreneur because you can't be one without all three.

Justin Tobin, DDG Inc

My parents used to tell me I could do and be anything I wanted to be, I was smart and could figure it out, they were always very supportive if I wanted to go 'off road' and not follow the crowd. They encouraged my crazy ideas and enjoyed hearing my logic if I came to a different outcome. Having such a strong foundation of support gave me the confidence and drive to pursue my interests and not be scared to fail. They never dwelled on me making mistakes, only on the lessons I learned from them so that I never repeated it again.

Paige Arnof-Fenn, Mavens & Moguls

My parents always told me that you don't have to go to school to be educated. Education is about curiosity, observation and exploration. They also taught me to question the rules, because rules are sometimes set by people who want things to stay the same or are set by bureaucrats whose goals may not be the best for everyone. An example of this thinking of learning to break the rules within reason was when I was in high school – on Mondays and Tuesdays I thought I wasn't learning much as the classes I had those two days did not have engaged teachers. I thought I would be able to learn the course on my own. My parents were completely fine with me skipping two days of school provided they could see I was using my time well. This taught me to confidently make my own decisions even if they were out of the norm or nonconformist. When I tell other people this story, they seem to think it's so out of the ordinary but for me this was so normal growing up.

Siddhi Mehta, Rhythm108

ASPIRATION

JODIE

When I was young, I wanted to be a checkout operator in a supermarket. I thought it would be great fun. I liked hearing the beep when items were scanned. I liked the idea of chatting to customers about their plans and what they were going to make with the ingredients they bought. Even more, I liked the idea of getting free food from the supermarket I was working in, though I had no proof that this was the case.

Fast forward to 2020. Jobs in retail in the USA have declined by 140,000 since January 2017[23] and automated self-checkouts are responsible for a large proportion of this number, not to mention online shopping. If my childhood ambitions had been the same when I left school, I'd have been entering a role with a short shelf-life.

I remember being sixteen and going to see the careers advisor at my school. If I had said then that I wanted to be a social media manager, I'd have had some strange looks. That job didn't exist. Facebook had only just been invented and was still called TheFacebook. Yet just six years later, I set up my own social media agency.

I'm always amazed when I talk to Uber drivers about self-driving cars and hear that they don't think they'll be mainstream for another twenty years, even though Uber is already running self-driving trials.[24]

A 2013 study carried out by Oxford University predicts that 47% of existing jobs in the United States are at risk of automation in the next twenty years.[25] Jobs and the demands and skills required of these jobs are changing incredibly quickly. Practise tying future aspirations with how much value can be added or how much of a difference can be made, or even just how much fun can be had. Tying career aspirations to specific job roles has little benefit because they simply might not exist in the future.

ACTIONABLES

- When you see someone in a specific role, ask 'Would you like to do that?'
- Talk about the day-to-day aspect of roles, including which ones might be enjoyable or challenging.
- Start discussions around how certain jobs might be carried out in the future.
- Ask, 'Could a robot do that job?'

I had a very happy childhood, and have very fond memories of growing up with my family but I saw both my parents work very hard, and I was conscious from a young age that money was tight at times. I can remember from a young age, maybe as young as five, thinking that when I was old enough to work, I would get the best paid job, and asking my dad who that was. Without putting a great deal of thought into it, he said the Prime Minister, so I went about as a child telling my family, much to their amusement, that I would become the Prime Minister. At some point over the years, I realised that while being the Prime Minister is certainly a well-paid job, it is not a role to aspire to purely for financial security. In retrospect, after beginning a career in investment banking, I continued to overweight the importance of money in my life. In stepping back from the industry, and setting up SBD, my focus was no longer on money but about creating the best product, promoting the sports that I loved, and building a brand that I was proud of and shared my values.

Ben Banks, SBD Apparel

I was raised to pursue success rather than specifically be an entrepreneur. Interestingly, of nine children, six of us started businesses and four of those have enjoyed pretty good success. The one phrase I remember from my childhood is, 'If you work for someone else you can be comfortable, but if you work for yourself you can be wealthy.'

Noel Farrelly, Tilney Group

My eight-year-old niece loves coming to my co-working space with me! I run my podcasting agency between Sydney and NYC so she has joined me in person and also by video call! When she faces a problem, I'm teaching her how to troubleshoot. We're also working on reverse engineering. She knows there are alternatives to being an employee and we talk about how she may end up in a field that hasn't even been invented yet.

Kelly Glover, The Talent Squad

SIR RICHARD BRANSON

Known for: Founder of Virgin

What else: In March 2000, Branson was knighted at Buckingham Palace for 'services to entrepreneurship'.

When Branson was a child he would often refuse to talk to adults, and cling to the back of his mother's skirt. His mother, Eve, worried his shyness would become debilitating as he got older and used some interesting techniques to prepare him for the future. According to an article on the Virgin website, Eve explained to her son that shyness is a form of selfishness. She said that being shy was merely thinking of oneself, rather than wanting to make other people happy. To bring him out of his shell, she'd encourage Branson and his sisters to perform skits and entertain their friends at dinner parties.

At the age of six, and after a shopping trip to a nearby village, Eve stopped the car about three miles from home and let her son out. She told him that he'd have to find his own way home by talking to people to ask for directions. He arrived home many hours later, but it worked and helped Branson develop a certain stoicism in the face of challenges. According to Branson, 'I started to become more comfortable interacting with adults and expressing myself.'

Branson said this approach 'has allowed me to chart an exciting path in life and in business.' He added, 'While some people would call her methods questionable – and I am by no means urging people to follow her example [...] they taught me what I consider to be life's greatest lesson: growth happens when you put yourself outside your comfort zone.'[26]

COMMITMENT

JODIE

When I was a student at the University of Sheffield, I joined the cross-country team. Our training for cross-country races, ten kilometres and half marathons involved a mix of short and long runs, track drills, fartlek training and hill sprints. Sheffield is a very hilly city. The whole team hated hill training and especially hated it when it was raining. Dragging yourself out of your cosy student house to run up hills in the pouring rain is no one's idea of fun, and it definitely wasn't mine.

I USED TO BE A WEATHER MAN

NOW I'M A WHETHER MAN

The cross-country coach didn't care if it was cold, or raining or hilly. He wanted us to commit to training in any weather conditions, so when we were hill training, he would have the whole team chant, 'We love the hills' as we were running up them. When it was raining, he had the whole team chant, 'We love the rain.' We'd chant it over and over again, for the entire training session. It helped eliminate any fair-weather excuses and it helped us see how silly an excuse 'it's raining' would be. It also, I'm sure, subliminally conditioned us to commit to training regardless of external circumstances.

In the Tim Ferriss book *Tools of Titans*, chess grandmaster and Brazilian jiu-jitsu black belt Josh Waitzkin inverses modern parenting norms around the weather to teach locus of control to his son. Waitzkin noticed unproductive language around the weather by parents, who labelled it as good or bad and used that to dictate their actions. Waitzkin explains, 'Jack and I never missed a single storm, rain or snow, to go outside and romp in it… We've developed this language around how beautiful it is. Now, whenever it's a rainy day, Jack says, "Look, Dada, it's such a beautiful rainy day," and we go out and we play in it.'[27]

What would happen if we stayed in every time it was raining? Or used the cold, or the heat, as an excuse not to do anything? We'd end up in a Goldilocks-type situation in which conditions had to be perfect in order to live our lives. We would abandon our commitments and surrender our progress to the hands of chance. It doesn't have to be that way.

ACTIONABLES

- You can apply this thinking to the world of an entrepreneur. Conditions to begin might never be perfect. There might always be political instability or a volatile exchange rate or a messy desk, but it's not important and shouldn't form an excuse not to get started. Commitment takes practice.

- Write your commitments down. Start each sentence with 'I promise I will...'

- Find the fun in the tough times. Associate pleasure with the challenge itself, and the feeling of overcoming it, not just with the easy bits.

- Don't use the weather as an excuse not to do anything.

- Pre-empt circumstances that might arise. Ask what they would do if x, y or z happens.

- Create the solutions for future problems. The list could include umbrellas, wellington boots, ice scrapers and sunglasses.

- Remind them of times when great things have happened upon committing and seeing something through.

My parents made me play outside all year round regardless of the weather. Their argument was that 'there is no such thing as bad weather, only bad clothing' (a common expression that is repeated time and time again to Swedish children). While I hated that saying as a child, it eventually taught me that there are some benefits to being prepared and equipped with the right tools. As an entrepreneur, this is something that has been particularly useful in order to stay ahead of the game.

Niklas Ingvar, Mentimeter

From an early age, my father ingrained in me to have the courage to follow my convictions. Today, as a father, I am instilling the same attitude and work ethic into my kids in addition to guiding them with a few things I've learned along the way. When you start looking at challenges as opportunities for personal development and growth, you set yourself up for success down the line. Have faith and be fearless.

Brad Beckerman, Stillhouse Spirits Co.

I have raised my children repeating four specific principles that they know off by heart. I have lived by them and have encouraged them to also. They are: turn up on time; say please and thank you; do what you say you will and finish what you start. Very few people do all four all of the time.

Noel Farrelly, Tilney Group

WHAT'S IN YOUR CONTROL?

JODIE

There's a stark difference between what is in your control and what is out of your control. Focusing on the former is powerful. You are in the driving seat of your life and you decide what you say and do and when you say and do it. Focusing on the latter is unhelpful and leads to frustration, anxiety and feeling powerless.

The earlier someone learns how to tell the difference between what is in their control and out of their control, the sooner their actions can be intentional and the sooner they can turn 'I want to' into 'I'm going to'. Identifying the difference begins the thought process of cause and effect because focusing on and actioning those things in your control will yield certain results. Focusing on and actioning things out of your control can't be done in the same way, so there's little point in spending energy there.

I was once eating at a seafood restaurant in downtown San Diego. A family of five was sitting on the next table. Everyone had received their food but the youngest daughter was waiting for her smoothie, which hadn't arrived. She told her mum that she wanted her smoothie. Her mum said, in a kind and gentle way, 'Well, what are *you* going to do about it?' Mum was trying to emphasise that the situation was in her daughter's control.

After some deliberation, the girl decided that it would be best to ask the server about her smoothie, but she was anxious to do so. Again, her mum said, 'Well, what are *you* going to do about it?' The girl said she'd like to practise, so together they acted out how the young girl would ask the server where her smoothie was. Once she had the confidence, the daughter went over and asked. The server apologised for forgetting and three minutes later the smoothie arrived. The girl's whole family congratulated her for working out what to do and having the courage to ask the question.

It was a simple question, asked in a gentle way, but wonderful to watch in practice. Use it wherever you see an opportunity: 'Well, what are *you* going to do about it?'

ACTIONABLES

Things in your control	Things out of your control
• What you say	• The weather
• How you respond	• How other people speak to you
• How much you learn	• What happens in the news
• How much you read	• What anyone else does
• How much you play	• How fast cars are driving
• How much help you ask for	

Using the examples above, look at what you are able to focus on and action:

🚀 'I want it to be sunny,' becomes, 'I'm going to prepare for rain too.'

🚀 'I want easy questions in my test,' becomes, 'I'll learn so I can answer any question.'

🚀 As a family, identify when something is in and out of your control.

In my family there was a lot of emphasis placed on personal responsibility and agency. In other words, we were always told that if there was something we didn't like or agree with, we had both a responsibility to change it and the ability to do so. This extended from everyday things like cleaning up after ourselves when we thought that the house was untidy, to larger issues, such as organizing volunteer initiatives at school. It's this feeling of responsibility and belief in my own potential to effect real change that drives me as an entrepreneur to this day. At its heart, entrepreneurship is based on wanting to see a different, better world.

Nikola Baldikov, Brosix

My father and mother both raised me to take responsibility and take action instead of complaining. If you made a mistake, learn from it and adapt. If something is out of your hands, focus on something that's within your control instead. They also taught me to not throw blame at people who work under me without first looking in the mirror. Perhaps they didn't get proper training, support or were a bad hire, which ultimately is something I can control the outcome of.

Travis Vengroff, Fool & Scholar Productions

COMPLAINING

JODIE

I remember being on holiday and seeing that another guest at the same hotel seemed to enjoy complaining. I saw him at dinner complaining that his table was wobbly. I saw him the following morning at breakfast, complaining that this table was also wobbly. The same thing happened at lunch. He just loved complaining and having a say about everything that was happening.

The next day I went down for breakfast and saw that half the tables were missing. Turns out they'd all been taken away to be 'de-wobbled'. Now the complainer had to wait longer to sit down for breakfast, and complained about that too.

If you look up Ben Nevis, the tallest mountain in the UK, on TripAdvisor, you'll see it has some 1* reviews. One of them complains that the mountain is 'far too big and takes far too long to climb'. Sometimes complaining can be funny, but mostly it's a drain.

One definition of complaining is 'describing an event or person negatively without indicating the next steps to fix the problem.'[28]

We've probably all been around a serial complainer and left their presence feeling uncharacteristically negative. It can be contagious. Spend too long in a negative, helpless mindset and it changes your inner voice. Changing your inner voice changes your thoughts, words and actions. It can change your present moment and therefore your past and your future.

'Never complain; never explain' was a maxim first coined by the British politician and prime minister Benjamin Disraeli,[29] and adopted as a motto by many other high-ranking Brits – from members of royalty to navy admirals and fellow prime ministers Stanley Baldwin and Winston Churchill.

The act of complaining implies that your (negative) judgement of something is important. It implies that things, even mountains, are there for us to judge. But what if they're not? What if they just exist? What if we were in the habit of seeing things just as they were without the need to form an opinion – just making the best of any situation? It's one thing to see a problem and create solutions to fix it, it's another to make a scene and love a grumble.

ACTIONABLES

There are two strategies to take complaining out of your day when you become aware that you or someone around you is complaining:

1. As soon as you become aware that it's happening, ask, 'What are you going to do about it?' This focuses the attention on the solution and ensures you don't get trapped in a maze of unhelpful thoughts.

2. Take the other handle. There's always another handle. So, a wobbly table becomes a fun game of twisting it around until it's stable or fashioning items to slide under one of its legs. A tall mountain becomes a great way to work up an appetite or to set a new record climb time.

We have strict policies on complaining. We don't talk about negative things unless necessary. They've never needed more than a reminder to adjust their behaviour if they're complaining. Begging, which is related to complaining, gets a warning, then a time-out.

Laura Hunter, LashLiner LLC

In our family, if a child whines or cries about having to do an everyday chore or responsibility (like getting dressed or unpacking a backpack), they have to choose something from the chore jar and get through that without negative reactions, lest they get another one.

> **Katie Kimball,** Kitchen Stewardship LLC and the Kids Cook
> Real Food eCourse

'I'll give you something to cry about' was a typical response to complaining.

> **John Frigo,** My Supplement Store

PART 2
ENTREPRENEURIAL SKILLS

DANIEL

'What do you do at work?' is a question all parents get asked eventually but some answers are easier than others. I imagine a fireman, police officer or nurse would have no problems explaining their work to a five-year-old, but what does an 'entrepreneur' actually do?

'I create a vision, take commercial risks, access resources, innovate products, recruit talent, make sales and steer my team towards high-performance' is an answer few adults would engage with, let alone a small person who's still unsure why gold coins are worth less than paper notes.

Entrepreneurship comprises a vast and varied set of skills but ultimately entrepreneurs do three key things:

1. Access resources beyond their current control.

2. Take on personal risks.

3. Innovate towards the commercial success of a venture.

Two out of three isn't really entrepreneurship. If you access resources and take personal risks but you are not striving for commercial success, you are probably a change-maker. If you run a successful business and access resources but there's no real risk to you, you are probably a business leader. If you make profit and take a risk with your existing resources, you are probably an investor. An entrepreneur does all three.

Kids are actually naturals when it comes to these things. Almost by definition, a baby must access resources beyond its control from day one to survive. Children are also amazing risk-takers and relentless in their pursuit of a goal. They do not care if they fall down a thousand times a week, they will keep trying until they learn to walk. They disregard warnings in their determination to get something they want, no matter how far out of reach it is placed. Turning your back on them for a few minutes is all it takes for them to identify a risky situation and embrace it.

The concept of risk and reward is not lost on the minds of little people. They quickly learn the concept of taking actions that lead to rewards. One only needs to bribe a child once with a sweet to discover that they will eat a new vegetable, but they normally won't do it again without a contract in place for more sweets. The first time you take a child around the neighbourhood on Halloween, you can watch as they put aside all fear in place of clear focus on the prize.

Even though entrepreneurship sounds like a complex topic, it is remarkably aligned to the inbuilt inclinations of a child and it's not difficult to channel that instinct towards a set of skills that will develop into business savvy when the time comes.

Children naturally come to see their parents as the source of all resources. Almost any decision that includes money, transport or supervision requires the involvement of the primary parent or guardian. There comes a point when it's important to encourage a shift in thinking so that children become resourceful themselves.

Developing skills is about building higher levels of resourcefulness. As it turns out, there are many ways that money can be accessed; there are many logistical solutions and many strategies for doing difficult things safely. As a child grows up and develops skills, they should see their parents as a potential solution rather than the only solution to their wants.

Going beyond the parents to get things done involves taking risks. Asking the neighbours if they want their car washed is full of risk – what if they say no, what if they aren't nice people, what if they aren't happy with the work or if the car gets damaged by accident? These are all risks you as a parent can help prepare your kids for as they acquire the skills to get paid for this job. If you do a good job, you can minimise the risks while also ensuring they feel a sense of ownership for the result.

Interacting with the real world and getting paid can be one of the most empowering moments in a young person's life. There's something magical about being handed 'real money' from someone other than your parents because you did something of value. I have met millionaires who barely bat an eyelid doing a large deal but beam when talking about the first time they ever got paid – that first payment is worth more to them than much larger sums.

When Jodie was twelve, she wanted a dog. She pleaded and begged for a puppy and pulled out every trick in the book to try and cajole her parents. Eventually, her father set her an assignment: he asked her to use Microsoft PowerPoint to create a 'pitch'. Jodie crafted her pitch based on the cuteness of dogs and other emotional benefits she saw fit to mention but failed to address the key concerns of her audience. The pitch was rejected.

Later, Jodie discovered that her cousin had been given a pet border collie and she was curious to find out how. It turns out that her cousin had also been asked to make a pitch but had focused on creating a dog-walking roster and giving an iron-clad guarantee that she would be responsible for cleaning up any mess the dog made. Having addressed the concerns of her target market, Jodie's cousin got buy-in for her four-legged start-up.

Today, Jodie is a successful entrepreneur with a social media agency. Having learned a valuable lesson, her team members never deliver a client pitch unless they know they are addressing the concerns and needs of their potential client. Jodie knows that a 'cute puppy' pitch might not be as powerful as a 'who's picking up the poop' pitch.

Entrepreneurial skills can be developed through many everyday interactions you have with your kids. As a parent or guardian, you can constantly sharpen important skills or shut them down. It's easy to condition a child not to even attempt to negotiate, not to ask for expensive items or never to talk to strangers. It takes a little more thought to develop the appropriate skills that accompany these situations. Nuanced situations can be tricky and as a busy parent you won't get it right every single time but it's worth the effort.

My father regularly found ways to teach me entrepreneurial skills. On most car journeys he would insist on listening to motivational or business-related tape sets. On one occasion, when I was about twelve years old, we were listening to a tape about marketing and the speaker was talking about the importance of having a clear 'call to action' in all marketing materials. This sparked a discussion analysing the billboards we drove past to see how many of them had met the criteria.

Years later, I was at a conference and heard the distinctive voice of the speaker from the tape set. I introduced myself and told him the story of me and Dad driving along looking at billboards based on his advice. We hit it off and went for a coffee. As a result of that conversation, I decided to move to London, where I met my wife and launched what would become a global business. I often think about how the tiniest things can steer the direction of life. More often than not, positive ideas and useful skills move life in the right direction.

In this section, you'll see how parents are fostering entrepreneurial skills in their kids. You'll see parents who are teaching their kids about strategy, sales, marketing, saving, investing, pitching, innovation and managing people. Like anything, these skills often start out as small tasks and build. Many of the world's most successful entrepreneurs learned their first business lessons before they were ten.

Even though I find it hard to accurately describe what I do for 'work' to my kids, I don't find it hard to share some of the skills that make it possible. It's wonderful to see them interacting and learning from real-world activities, knowing that little steps today will compound into big capabilities over time.

PRACTICE

JODIE

There are four stages involved in progressing from incompetence to competence in a skill. They are:

1. Unconscious incompetence: when you don't know that you're not skilled at something; perhaps before you've tried.

2. Conscious incompetence: when you know that you're not skilled at something; perhaps after you try once.

3. Conscious competence: when you are skilled at something but it requires your focus and attention; like when becoming proficient at a skill.

4. Unconscious competence: when you are so skilled at something that it feels second nature; when you have mastered a skill.

Observing someone operating with unconscious competence can be awe-inspiring. Ballet dancers, musicians, someone confidently and effectively running a meeting, speaking on stage or even deftly running a school lesson. Every person reaching unconscious competence in a skill has gone through the journey described to reach their level of mastery. Each level involves practice. Conscious, definite, purposeful practice.

For me, this means that when I'm learning to be excellent at something, I make sure I give it my full attention. I'll reserve time in my diary for it. I'll turn my phone off and ensure I'm not going to be disturbed. Full commitment enables conscious practice that leads to unconscious competence.

It's important in work and leisure alike. In any workplace, doing nearly any role, over time you develop expertise and can solve each arising challenge easier than you did before. It doesn't happen straight away, it develops. In a work role, the people who are excellent at what they do often get promoted within a company until they are in charge of people or processes. In the world of self-employment, people who get really good at honing their craft are seen as experts in their industry or they can couple their expertise with production and build an empire.

For both children and grown-ups, having the experience of becoming good at something might give them the confidence that they require to go on and be good at something else. Seeing the results that practice brings can be powerful, it leads to an understanding of cause and effect – calculated and definite inputs that lead to specific outcomes. It makes for a good example to point at in the future, for example: 'Remember when you didn't want to practise your violin, and then you did and then you passed your grade four and it felt amazing? You *are* capable.'

On Technium founder Kevin Kelly's sixty-eighth birthday, he published a fascinating article called '68 Bits of Unsolicited Advice'.[30] One bit of advice concerned mastery and was far more practical advice than 'follow your dreams' or similar: 'Following your bliss is a recipe for paralysis if you don't know what you are passionate about. A better motto for most youth is "master something, anything". Through mastery of one thing, you can drift towards extensions of that mastery that bring you more joy, and eventually discover where your bliss is.'

ACTIONABLES

- Create a structure of learning together. It could be about anything. Dinosaurs, trains, cars, schoolwork or whatever they show an interest in.

- Attend swimming lessons, music lessons or learn how to ride a bike or do keepie-uppies.

- Whatever the exercise is, commit to the practice. Recognise and draw attention to milestones.

- Film before and after. With keepie-uppies, someone filmed at the start, then after ten minutes of practice, then after two hours of practice, will have noticeably developed in the skill.

- Keep a log of before and after. Write down someone's expertise on day one, then keep progress markers so you can track how far you have come with practice.

- Create a thirty-day challenge. Commit to practising this activity for thirty minutes every day and keep a record of progress made.

When I was younger, I was encouraged by my parents to continually improve my dancing through practice. They taught me that it was OK to make mistakes as long as in doing so I learned and adapted what I did. Practising various dance routines with my sister was not only fun but it enabled me to hone my technical and artistic skills to go on to further training and ultimately enter the profession. So, put in maximum effort, don't be frightened of going wrong and remember to, as my mum would say, 'Jump and the net will appear!'

Jessica Wheeler, Elmhurst Ballet School

When I was young, I told my dad I wanted to be a singer. He said, 'You need some good singer role models then.' At the time I was listening to bubble-gum pop, and he didn't think that was good enough. I remember that he brought home the cassette tapes of Mariah Carey, Whitney Houston and Celine Dion. Later on, we started listening to Christina Aguilera. He said, 'These are women who can really sing, you need to be like these women.' He also told me that Mariah Carey had really bad stage fright, but she overcame that because she had this incredible voice, a story that definitely had an impression on me. These women became my role models and I channelled them whenever I sang. I was also encouraged to sing in front of my family. My big Greek family would come round and my dad would say, 'Lydia's going to be a singer – she wants to sing for you,' so I would perform for them. I now don't have a fear of speaking or performing in front of people, and it must have come from that experience because it was just seen as the norm. While I never made it as a singer, music gave me huge confidence in myself, probably more than I realise.

Lydia Papaphilippopoulos-Snape, Warwick Street Kitchen

I was encouraged to practise different sports and activities and not be fixated only in doing one so I could have a vast amount of experiences and focus on the ones I felt more inclined to, due to talent, pleasure and fit. I think trying different things is at the heart of being an entrepreneur because very often you won't find your passion or true calling at first, and even when you do, growing in business requires a vast set of knowledge and experiences, exactly the opposite than being a 'specialist' in only one area.

This experience also took place when I started taking on summer jobs and paid activities from fourteen and fifteen years onwards. I worked as a martial arts instructor, bartender, waiter, activities organizer and English business conversational teacher. The latter allowed me to help a Spanish businessman needing to practise English and wanting to pay less than a full-price teacher to improve his fluency. It required me to understand the world behind insurance and re-insurance at age eighteen, which is quite complex but I found intriguing. Practising different activities and getting engaged in different areas honed my curiosity and helped me become who I am today. I am really grateful for my mother for always encouraging me to have new experiences and not be afraid of the unknown.

Jonathan Aeschlimann, DIV Brands

The skill of learning, and the skill of mastery, can develop independently of whatever you're learning or mastering. That's why learning music is so useful. It teaches mastery. It teaches practice. If you can learn music, you can learn anything. No matter what your kid gets fascinated with, encourage them on the mastery path. Skateboarding, dancing, acting, whatever. In learning how to be great at it, they'll learn how to be great at anything else, too.

Derek Sivers, sive.rs

THINKING OF IDEAS

JODIE

Being able to think of good ideas can open up so many future opportunities. It's also an impressive skill to master for someone of any age. In his book *Choose Yourself!* author James Altucher introduces the concept of ideas being a form of currency.[31] I see it in practice at my social media agency. In a sales process, anyone we're pitching against might be roughly level with us on how well they present, how much experience they have and how personable they are in meetings. What will, without fail, make the difference in winning a new client is the strength of the ideas we put forward. So that's what my team focuses on: having better ideas than anyone else.

Altucher's book goes on to explain how someone can get really good at this by becoming what he calls an 'ideas machine'. Put simply, this daily practice involves thinking up ten ideas every day, for anything at all. You don't need to keep the ideas and you certainly don't need to implement them. The magic is in the practice itself. This might be ideas around what to write for a blog post, what to do with your Saturday or how Ben & Jerry's could sell more ice cream. It doesn't matter what the ideas are – what matters is that the practice happens daily and that you keep going until you think of ten. Why ten? Because the first four or five are easy. It's the sixth, seventh and final few that really stretch your ideas muscle to the point where it's adapting and getting better at the process.

The earlier you start, the better an ideas machine you can become. Further to this, having a follow-up discussion about the feasibility of each idea can help develop a framework for decision making.

ACTIONABLES

Think of ten ideas for:

- Where to go this weekend
- Making grandma's birthday special
- Keeping your bedroom tidy
- Breakfasts this week
- Computer games you could create
- The routes you could walk to school
- Bedtime stories to write
- Things to do outside when it rains
- How your local convenience store could attract more customers
- Making the most of warm weather

I encourage my eleven-year-old to think about the products and services that surround her, and we regularly discuss advertising ideas. I discuss my ideas that haven't worked with my business and what I have learned from them. I hope to teach my children to be able to adjust adequately and think on their feet – key skills when becoming an entrepreneur.

Libby James, Merchant Advice Service

My immigrant father unintentionally raised me to be an entrepreneur. He would play a driving game with me and my younger brother: What business would you put there? We'd drive by derelict plazas and empty lots and he would prompt me to think about the surrounding area and put a business there. If I got lazy and answered something generic like 'a restaurant' he'd click his tongue in annoyance and expected me to elaborate – which type, formal, casual, franchise, new, etc.

Lynda Correa Peralta, Pocket Palette

Growing up in an entrepreneurial household one lesson really stuck with me and helped instil an entrepreneurial spirit in me, and that is 'you have to take the initiative'. The truth is every person has ideas, ideas that if implemented properly could make a great business. But few have the initiative to implement those ideas and see them through. My dad always used to say, 'Thoughts are only good when you put them into action.' You will never have every answer, know exactly what is going to happen, or be guaranteed success, but you have to put the idea into practice or it will never go anywhere.

My parents were never afraid to not only discuss ideas for new businesses, but actually implement them and I got to see that process in action. Not every one of them succeeded, but being an entrepreneur doesn't mean everything you do succeeds; it means you work to make your ideas a success.

Jacob Weil, RMS Accounting

SARA DAVIES MBE

Known for: Founder of Crafter's Companion

What else: The youngest person to become a dragon on BBC Two's *Dragons' Den*.

Davies grew up in a small pit village in the northeast of England to parents who both ran businesses, although they never would have used the term 'entrepreneur' because it felt too big and fancy. She recalls that her dad seemed to have a new idea for a business every year, doing everything from double glazing sales to setting up a bike shop, where he paid Sara and her sister 20p per wheel to get all of the rust off.

Davies and her sister were very involved in these businesses and Sara grew up thinking of business as a way of life, a 24/7 commitment and part of your personality and being. Despite holding dreams of becoming a history teacher when she grew up, Davies chose business studies at GCSE level. She said that even as a teenager business felt natural to her, like common sense, and she'd enjoy talking about the subject with her dad to gain real-life context. She felt excited to see her parents working hard to build businesses and she never felt frightened of hard work herself. When she was eighteen, she decided that she didn't want to be a history teacher, she wanted to be in business.

Davies opted to study business studies at York University with a view to taking what she had learned and applying it to the family's various companies. Within her course she spent a year in industry, where she worked in a small craft company – an experience she described as eye-opening. Davies was able to apply the models and processes she had learned from her degree into her business role and remembers she absolutely loved doing so.[32]

WHY A BUSINESS EXISTS

JODIE

Many businesses define what they do and why they do it in a *mission statement.* This sets out their overriding purpose which fosters alignment within the company and understanding from its customers. Some examples from well-known companies include:

- Tesla: To accelerate the world's transition to sustainable energy.
- IKEA: To create a better everyday life for the many people.
- TED: To spread ideas.
- Apple: Bringing the best user experience to its customers through its innovative hardware, software and services.

For smaller and lesser-known businesses, their mission statement might not be so clearly communicated, but they likely exist:

- To provide a service that people need.
- To solve a problem.
- To contribute towards a bigger mission.
- To create a specific outcome for a specific group of people.

Understanding what a business is there to do can help ignite the thought process of which businesses are needed or which ones will be a success. Who knows, this thought process could lead to your son or daughter starting the next Tesla or Apple.

Prompting discussions about the topics below will develop commercial awareness that will soon begin to happen unconsciously, and entrepreneurial thinking will follow with this commercial awareness as its foundation.

ACTIONABLES

Think of the five businesses you come into contact with the most and see if you can find their mission statements. Discuss:

- Whether you think they are succeeding in their mission
- Any alternative suggestions

When in a cafe, restaurant, bar, cinema, store or place of work, etc, discuss:

- What the business is there to do
- Who it serves and why it's important to them
- How it could serve them better
- What you would change if you were the owner
- Whether you would like to own such a business (and why or why not)

When using a service, for example, a hairdresser or cleaner, discuss:

- What that person is here to do, and for whom
- Who pays this person to do their work
- What would happen if this person wasn't here doing their job
- What would happen if this person did their job badly

Think about your road, local high street or town and discuss:

- Which business you would love to see set up at the end of your road and why
- How often you would buy from it
- Who else would buy from it
- Whether that business would be able to stay there for a long time
- How far people would travel to buy from that business

I believe the first step to instilling an entrepreneurial spirit in my kids is making sure they are informed on what's going on in the world so they can decide what they are passionate about. We receive the print edition of the paper every day and we use it to spark family discussion once we're all back home together. I look at the pictures with my girls and tell them about the headlines of the day, often picking stories with pictures of food, travel, retail and houses to talk about what problems featured companies are trying to solve, asking them if they think that's a good idea or not.

Kimmie Greene, Intuit QuickBooks

As a small business owner, I am lucky enough to have so many hands-on experiences to share with my children about being an entrepreneur. From order fulfilment, to marketing, to customer service – my kids are able to see and understand how each piece comes together, and every aspect has its importance in running a successful business.

Kim, Mama Java Coffee

My father had his own accounting firm and he always wanted to invest in very unique ideas. His clients were also entrepreneurs and we would talk about what they did and how they became a client. I was young when my interest in business took hold and wanting to be like my father had everything to do with it. Since he spoke of business on his car phone and always worked late at home after office hours that is how I bonded with him, asking what his client was talking about and that's what got me into being a businessman myself.

Dan Wachtel, Harbour Capital Partners

SUPPLY AND DEMAND

JODIE

I will always remember my economics teacher reciting, 'Supply and demand, supply and demand, supply and demand' over and over again in lessons. Although he did this on purpose, in a comical way, it demonstrated that supply and demand is a fundamental concept in economics and, therefore, business.

Without supply and demand, business does not exist. I feel so strongly that everyone should have a grasp of this concept that we devoted a section of one of the Clever Tykes stories to it. In *Code-it Cody*, teacher Mr Chip explains to the Computer Club members that it's paramount to create something that people want to buy. He uses the example of a computer game company that produces games so popular that there are queues outside the video game store when each new version is released.

Appreciating that there must be demand or a market for a product or service is the basis of a business plan for any idea someone might have. Knowing who will want that product defines the target audience – it all leads to a deeper understanding of the business world.

Whether running a business or working within one, commercial awareness is important. It leads to someone making better decisions and being able to second-guess a good move for the business or the people within it. In my agency, having commercial awareness means someone can suggest a way forward that is planned out and backed up by a solid understanding of what a business is there to do.

Demand isn't always obvious; it might require deeper thinking. Try and work this out:

ORANGES VERSUS CLEMENTINES

I wanted something sweet to eat, so I went to the fruit section at the supermarket and decided between an orange and a clementine.

The orange costs less than the clementine. The orange is bigger than the clementine

The orange is tastier than the clementine. But I bought the clementine. *Why?*

[See below the Actionables section for the answer.]

ACTIONABLES

Here are some everyday examples to invite discussion about supply, demand and commercial awareness. I've given some suggestions of answers and discussion points below each one, although these are not exhaustive and the conversation could take a different direction.

- Why are we standing in a queue?

- How could the queue be made shorter?

- What other option does someone have for buying what they need?

- Why might they choose this shop?

Suggestions: People are prepared to wait to make their purchase or they have already spent time walking around the store; the queue could be made shorter by opening another cashier, having longer opening hours or serving people faster; they could buy somewhere else or online; they might choose the shop because it's close to their house or work or has a good reputation.

- Why do people want ice cream when the weather is hot?

- What could ice cream vans do in the winter?

- How does the ice cream van know how much ice cream to buy?

Suggestions: They want it to cool them down or they might want it because everyone else is having one; in the winter they could sell hot drinks or hot food or they could travel to a different warmer place; they might base their predictions on last year's sales or on the weather forecast.

🚀 How many lessons can a music teacher give each week?

🚀 How could they see more students?

🚀 How could they make more money?

Suggestions: Take shorter breaks between classes, work for longer each day, hold lessons at their house or hold group classes, sell music books, learn more instruments, teach classes online or charge students more.

'Oranges versus clementines' answer: Because a clementine is easier to peel. The value gained from it being easier to peel outweighs the price, size and taste factors.

To help my daughter (age seventeen) understand what goes into a business, whenever she comes up with a business idea, I take her through the steps to see if it's viable and can make money. We discuss who will buy the product or service, what customers were doing before the product or services existed, and why does she think people will really want it. Then we talk about the production costs, marketing costs and try to identify who will do each of the things to make the business successful. And, of course, I tell her that if we can figure all of this out, I would invest in it and help her out. Once she sees how much research, preparation and hard work is required, she tends to abandon the idea. This repeats about every four months.

Marty Schultz, Blindfold Games

I encourage my two sons to ask, 'Why?' when they encounter a business – from small ones in the neighborhood, to the mid to large ones we see in advertising. We play the 'Four Ps' game and break down a business by their product, price, place and promotion to see how all of the pieces work together. This allows us to understand how math works into everyday life (how many 'units' does a business have to sell daily, weekly, monthly to break even?).

Clint White, WiT Media

My family owned a restaurant that sold sandwiches – subs. When I was in middle school (grades six to eight) I would make my own sub for lunch each day. As you typically do, I would cut the 12" sub in half to make it easier to eat. However, I also cut one half of the sandwich into three parts that were 2" each. Since school cafeteria lunches are so bad, it was easy to sell half of my lunch for $2 for each of those three parts. I would collect $6 for half of a sub that sold for that price outside the school.

My supply of subs was valued more highly in the school cafeteria because the supply was extremely limited. Only three people would be eating a sub for lunch, everyone else would have the mystery meat served by the school cafeteria. Outside the school cafeteria, the supply was virtually unlimited. Anyone could stop by the restaurant and buy a 12" sub for about $6. Here in the school, I sold a 6" portion of that sub for the same $6. Before I graduated to selling sub sandwiches in middle school, I got my start selling candy on the bus in elementary school. I bought the bulk candy at a membership club and sold it for $0.25 per piece. Here too, I leveraged supply and demand to double or triple my money. These were not explicit lessons from my family, but the side effect of being raised in an entrepreneurial family. Before I was in the sixth grade, I was calculating food cost, reading P&L (profit and loss) reports, and developing bookkeeping systems in MS Excel. By the time I learned what supply and demand was, I had already been leveraging it for years.

Frank Jones, OptSus Marketing

REFLECTION

JODIE

I remember writing a school holiday journal. It was A4 and the top half of each page was plain and the bottom half was lined. I used the top to draw a picture of what I had done that day, and the bottom to explain it. I really enjoyed thinking about what I had done or achieved or learned and putting it into picture and caption format.

Now I realise that making journaling a daily practice led me to review each day and helped me to not waste any. Perhaps subconsciously, I began to feel that every day had to count, because otherwise I wouldn't have anything to write down. It also opened up conversations about what I wanted to do tomorrow, how else I could spend my time, and if I had enjoyed the day's happenings. In other words, I was aware of my day-to-day and able to make decisions for myself.

Daily journaling can also lead to a heightened sense of gratitude. I would always focus on the good things that happened each day. Those things that made me smile or think. It's been well documented that gratitude practice in itself is linked to lower stress and other health benefits. From entrepreneur Arianna Huffington's book *Thrive*, 'According to a study by researchers from the University of Minnesota and the University of Florida, having participants write down a list of positive events at the close of a day – and why the events made them happy – lowered their self-reported stress levels and gave them a greater sense of calm at night.'[33]

Because journaling and practising gratitude trains the brain to focus on positivity and helps someone live in the present instead of the past or future, it can form a solid foundation from which someone goes about their day-to-day. Imagine how powerful doing this from a young age can be in setting someone up for a happy and fulfilled future.

ACTIONABLES

🚀 Put each day up for review. Ask questions such as, 'What did you enjoy today?' and, 'What did you learn today?'

🚀 Each night before bed, list the three things you are most grateful for. These could be people, places or events from the day. They could be aspects of nature, good things that have happened to other people or even the weather.

🚀 As a step further, write down each day's 'three things I'm grateful for' somewhere you can read them again in the future.

🚀 Even when mistakes are made or things don't go to plan, discuss why you are still grateful. (The answers might include the chance to learn, the chance to do better next time or the chance to do something else.)

My daughter and I 'debrief' at the end of every day. We talk about what I 'do' during the day, who I had meetings with, what the meeting was about, why did I go to the meeting, and if I met anyone new. As well, did I create something? A blog post, a social media post, a new collaboration, a podcast. I think it's important for my children to know that mommy doesn't just disappear and go to a nonconceptual location known to them only as 'work'. In return, she often tells me that she had meetings with her dolls or a friend and they discussed very important work, or created a work of art or a picture that will make someone happy to receive!

Coreyne Woodman-Holoubek, Contracted Leadership

I used to keep a diary when I was a child. It helped me realize what I valued and what felt true to me. I believe that having the chance to re-read your experiences and thoughts is good emotional management.

Kalina Stoyanova, Independent Fashion Bloggers

Journaling and keeping a diary I think helped express those things that were inside my head but I felt no one else around me would ever understand. I didn't feel like I ever fit in so expressing those thoughts on paper, the things I wanted to do with my life, felt freeing and opened a lot of creative thinking.

Charline Bucher, Time As This LLC

SARA BLAKELY

Known for: Founder of Spanx

What else: In 2012, *Forbes* named her as the youngest female self-made billionaire in the world at age forty-one.

When Blakely first told her friends and family about the concept of Spanx, 'they looked horrified!'[34] Each night at dinner, Blakely and her brother were invited by their father to share their failures from the day. Instead of being disappointed, angry or upset, he would celebrate their attempts. 'What it did was reframe my definition of failure,' Sara told Business Insider.

'Failure for me became not trying versus the outcome... My dad would encourage me any time something didn't go the way I expected it to, or maybe I got embarrassed by a situation, to write down where the hidden gifts were and what I got out of it. I started realising that in everything there was some amazing nugget that I wouldn't have wanted to pass up.'[35]

PLANNING AHEAD

JODIE

For as long as I can remember, whenever I've been away I have packed my own suitcase. Perhaps I was four when it first happened. I knew we were leaving for a trip the next day, and my mum instructed me to go and pack my things so I'd have everything I needed. To me, it was normal. Who else would pack it?

It's only now that I realise this *isn't* the norm, that I've thought about what it taught me growing up.

It might not sound like a life-changing event, just packing for a trip, but from a young age it actually taught me every skill I use today. It taught me how to plan for the future, even if that future was just a weekend at grandma's. It taught me how to work within a constraint. The suitcase was only so big, and there definitely wasn't any spare room in my sister's. It taught me critical thinking. What was I doing? What would I need? What was my priority and which sacrifices did I need to make? It taught me independence and decision making because no one else was going to decide for me. It taught me about learning from my mistakes, the mistakes I made when packing for previous trips.

Looking back, I now attribute this as a large factor in everything I've ever achieved, in my whole life and career. Every milestone, every award, every success has been down to the fact that when I was a small child, whenever our family went on holiday, my mum made me pack my own suitcase.

ACTIONABLES

- Create a written packing inventory. Ask them to make a list of what they will need, then pack based on the list.

- Trial and error. Let them pack their suitcase unassisted and see how well they do.

- Have them lay everything out on the floor before putting items in their case.

- Ask questions. When will they need items they have picked? Are there substitutes that could be made?

- Upon one successful packing endeavour, write a list of what was included and use it for reference next time.

- Living with decisions. As grown-ups we can't pack too much because we need to carry it ourselves. Think about how you can ensure the decisions they make have relevance to future responsibility.

I include my son in money discussions. When I took him on vacation to Los Angeles it cost $40 per night to park at our hotel. There was a parking garage right next to our hotel that charges $15 per night to park there. I parked in the parking garage next to our hotel. Ryan complained about having to walk over to the hotel. I explained that it was $25 cheaper to park next door and over six days that would save us $150 which meant I would have an extra $150 to spend on fun stuff on vacation. Ryan agreed with me to park next door and spend the extra $150 on fun stuff instead of wasting the money. When we go on vacation, I give Ryan money in advance that he can spend on whatever he wants. I cover the basics like food and hotel but if he wants a toy or a game, he has to budget his own money and decide what he wants to buy. And he has to pay all by himself which means he has to work out how much the item will cost, add in taxes (I help with that), hand the money to the cashier and make sure he gets the proper change back.

Alexandra Axsen, Lake Okanagan Realty Ltd

I grew up in a pretty religious family, and one of the rules was that I wasn't allowed to use my computer on a Sunday. I'd go to church in the morning and come back home longing for an afternoon playing Sid Meier's Colonization – the must-have strategy game of the time – but I wasn't allowed, so I improvised. In the week, I'd make notes on things in the game, and then when Sunday came, instead of playing, I would spend the day obsessing over my notes and the 135-page game manual, planning out all the possible permutations and strategies that I was going to explore during the week.

As I moved from loving games to loving writing software, I took this a step further, writing out whole programs on Sunday afternoons, which I'd then type up as soon as I got home from school on Monday. In fact, I came to really enjoy this method! When I completed my degree in computer science, in a time before laptops were affordable to a student, I wrote up my whole 400-file-long final year project on sheets of A4, while sitting in my favourite coffee shop, then went to the labs in the evenings and typed it up. To this day, I try and delay coding my software for as long as possible, letting the program form in my mind over time before casting finger to keyboard.

The other great huge effect of this is that as a businessman I'm assiduous about planning things out in detail before getting started. I'm always driven by developing in-depth long-term strategies, rather than being reactive. The fact that I had to stop every week and just have a day to think and plan has been hugely defining in the way I think, and I consider it a huge positive. Although try telling that to my ten-year-old self!

Jeremy Walker, Thalamus AI

USING THE PHONE

JODIE

MUMMY! MUMMY!
THE LADY ON THE PHONE
IS TRAINING
PORPOISES

Entrepreneurs have to be great communicators. It's a key part of much that they do. Pitching, selling, leading a team and building a rapport with clients and partners. Learning how to be great on the phone forms part of this communication.

When the phone rang in my family home, it was exciting. Hearing the ring triggered a race we were all part of, for the first person to shout, 'I'll get it' and run to the handset. We loved the idea that someone was calling to speak to us and we were eager to hear who it was.

Mostly, it was one of my mum's friends. We didn't have caller ID so I wouldn't know who was calling until they started talking, but when I picked up, even before they asked, 'Is your mum there?' they would always ask how I was and we'd have a chat about school or hobbies or pets. Talking to grown-ups was a normal occurrence and answering the phone was no big deal.

Since running a business, I have met (and hired) people who really don't like answering the phone or talking on the phone, especially when someone else can hear them. A 2019 survey of UK office workers found that 40% of baby boomers and 70% of millennials experience anxious thoughts when the phone rings.[36] You may have experienced this yourself. It's so easy to hide behind emails, WhatsApp and social media and never make calls. However, it's the calls and face to face encounters that really help you get to know the people who might become your clients and colleagues.

Without caller ID, a phone ringing has unknown entities that could be intimidating to anyone. Who is calling? Why are they calling? What do they want? Even with caller ID, we might not know *why* someone is calling. Being able to confidently answer a phone and deal with the request made of us develops skills in preparedness and the ability to think on our feet, which are useful for any endeavour.

Answering the phone is one thing. Making outbound calls is another. While I'm certain no one really likes cold calling, being able to make a call and clearly deliver or ask for the necessary information is an essential part of everyday life, not just for entrepreneurs. Practising with routine calls like booking doctor or dentist appointments can provide valuable practice without the risk of much going wrong. I don't remember ever attending a doctor or dentist's appointment I hadn't called up to book myself. Who else would book it for me? I realise now that my mum saw it as a way of building confidence and independence.

ACTIONABLES

To develop phone confidence in making or receiving calls:

- Teach them which button to press to answer and hang up.
- Let them choose the ringtone.
- Practise different greetings so they can use the one they like the most.
- Play it down – answering the phone isn't an issue.

- 🚀 Practise conversing. Role-play the phone ringing and take it in turns to be the caller.
- 🚀 Be there to support. Use loudspeaker the first few times until confidence develops.
- 🚀 Tell your friends you're practising telephone skills so they know to join in when your son or daughter answers.
- 🚀 Cover every eventuality. Teach them how to take a message or what to say before they pass the phone over to you.
- 🚀 Start small. Help them to book routine doctor or dentist appointments first.

As small children we were encouraged to answer the phone and also make phone calls. I can remember back when I was nine years old my mum was in hospital. I wanted to call to speak with her and so my dad said that I needed to make that call myself. I needed to talk with the hospital reception, share her name and room number and ask to speak with her. At the time it was a scary experience, but it was through regular practice with conversations like this that I became confident in talking with adults and seeking out information I needed.

Meryl Johnston, Bean Ninjas

It was our role to answer the phone when it rang. It taught us the value of speaking to strangers and handling conversations. My brother and I also had to place orders when we were little at restaurants, etc. Or, I remember being six years old and we were driving across the USA before we lived in Australia. As we drove to each motel, it was my and my brother's job to go up and ask if they had a room for the night and what the rates were.

Mike Clark, Key Person of Influence QLD

I remember being fascinated with phones as a young child. This was when phones still had good old dial plates and it took some force to dial the higher numbers. My parents were amused because I kept calling random people – the concept of phone books completely escaped me. Later, I delighted in playing the 'phone butler' and taking messages for my parents. As a teenager, I took a part-time job as a market research assistant, where I had to call people up for phone interviews. It was really interesting, and I loved the challenge of persuading people who had previously declined, to take part in our studies after all.

Sabine Harnau, From Scratch Communications

MANAGING A CALENDAR

JODIE

One of the most popular articles I've ever written is called 'Stop Acting Like You're Going To Live Forever'. As adults, we become increasingly aware of our rapidly decreasing time left on this planet. As kids we have absolutely no idea.

On one hand, there's something wonderful about having a carefree existence, with the belief that your days are endless and you have all the time in the world. On the other hand, not seeing time as a finite resource can lead to truly wasting it.

I once read about a father who reminded himself every day, 'One day she'll go to college.' When his daughter eventually did, he was pleased that he had been able to make the absolute most of his time with her. Eighteen years can fly by.

PLAY DATE?
OK IVE GOT A
3-4 NEXT SATURDAY...

Getting really good at planning means that time is made the most of by all involved. It leads to consciously choosing how you spend your time in favour of flitting it away and then wondering where it went. It doesn't need to be a full calendar of activities, excursions or obligations – even an awareness of how long someone has available to them each week is a useful exercise.

In one of the Clever Tykes storybooks, *Walk-it Willow*, Willow starts a dog-walking business and to organise her customers she uses a calendar. It transforms Willow from feeling disorganised and out of control to her ruling the day and being the master of her time.

ACTIONABLES

- Display a weekly planner on the fridge or somewhere that everyone can see it and encourage contributions.

- Give your kids their own calendars to write things they want to do.

- Talk to them about all the things they list and about how they can plan them.

- Give suggestions. When shall we go for a walk? What would you like for dinner on Thursday? How can we prepare for an event in advance?

- Allow more time. Include travel time, pit-stop time and leave enough time for the activity to extend.

- Talk about trade-offs so they understand if you do one thing, it means you can't do another.

Time management is a skill rarely proactively taught. Make organisational skills a focus by giving your kids their own calendars to keep track of family events, school project due dates, extracurricular activities, so they can begin to understand prioritising their own commitments and responsibilities. Show your children how to think about the future, not just the present. Beyond time management, being able to understand that what you do now will impact you later is crucial. Get together to map out the week ahead and then see what your children can do now to help lighten the load later.

Inger Ellen Nicolaisen, Nikita Hair

I'm also teaching them about balance. By watching me balance my business with spending time with them, I'm teaching them a very important lesson in entrepreneurial life – work hard, play hard. They see me put down the notebook, walk away from the computer, and go play outside with them – and I'm confident this helps to create well-rounded entrepreneurs of the future!

Kim, Mama Java Coffee

RESPONSIBILITY

JODIE

Taking responsibility is about ownership of tasks and commitment to doing them well. It's also about wanting to be in charge of something instead of wanting someone else to do it for you. While someone might seem to naturally want more responsibility, I believe it can also be taught and learned. Responsibility builds upon independence to give it purpose and direction.

Responsibility versus independence:

🚀 Independence is being able to walk home from school on your own. Responsibility is sticking to the right route.

🚀 Independence is packing your own suitcase.
Responsibility is taking ownership of packing it well.

🚀 Independence is being left to your own decisions.
Responsibility is working out the right ones to make.

When working alongside people, I have found that one of the most valuable things someone can do is what they say they are going to do. In any career, those who are able to practise and demonstrate responsibility are those who are given more responsibility.

As an entrepreneur, no one follows you up to make sure you've completed your tasks or made your phone calls or delegated and assigned the actions that will make your business a success. The great ideas in your head remain ideas until you take responsibility for turning them into reality. Doing all of this and doing it well might lead to having a career you love, a great reputation and achieving success in your work and life. Even if someone's future aspirations don't involve huge responsibility, it will help them do whatever they choose to the best of their abilities, resulting in higher levels of satisfaction and purpose. Shirking responsibilities means losing business and being chased by your accountant, or worse. When something is in your care, the repercussions of not following through with your actions can be severe.

ACTIONABLES

Each of these tasks can be practised at home and while out, from a young age:

- Taking complete ownership of tasks.
- Seeing jobs through to completion.
- Being accountable for a job's success.
- Cultivating resilience and taking responsibility for overcoming obstacles.
- Committing to a responsibility over a long period of time.

Here are some ways you can help responsibility be learned:

- Model responsibility. Tell them about the responsibilities you have while you are actioning them. Talk about *why* you are doing what you are doing.
- Practise 'If this, then that'. If there's ice on the windscreen, then what needs to happen? If we leave the house, then how do we make sure it's secure?
- Invite assistance with your responsibilities, starting as young as possible. Folding sheets is a two-person job, as laying a table, cooking or cleaning can be.
- Be patient with results. The most important thing is the completion of the task, the second is how well it's completed. Take care that focusing on perfection doesn't overshadow the accomplishment of completion.
- Specifically give them something to be responsible for, like a plant or chore, or even a younger sibling if age-appropriate. Assigning tasks and responsibilities and then following them up might just help someone commit and see something through. Even better is helping them to *proactively* work out what needs to be done and take responsibility for that without prompting.

When I was a kid, my parents were conservative entrepreneurs. They both worked full-time professional jobs and we owned two self-service car washes as their side gig. Whenever we had problems at school with academics or school policies, my dad would say, 'Don't ever let any other mere mortal tell you how you have to live your life. If you don't like it, do something about it.' And so I did. I put together petitions to change our school uniform, I organized a fundraiser when I was told it was too big a job for a teenager, and I rearranged my class schedule to accommodate a health problem in my senior year of high school. My parents let me do it myself. They didn't step in to fight my battles for me. But my dad read that petition and helped me re-word it. My mom gave me phone numbers for people to help with that fundraiser. They both encouraged me to be my own advocate for my health that last year of high school. Never once did they offer to take over those tasks for me. But man did they cheer me on in a big way.

That kind of confidence in the abilities of your kids is key to fostering an entrepreneurial spirit. If your parents believe in the inevitability of your success, it's easy for you to believe in it too.

Ruth Rau, Mouse Loves Pig

I never really discussed entrepreneurism directly with my children, but somehow, they all are doing just that. There are definitely some things we did while our kids were growing up to foster a sense of entrepreneurism: Don't be a helicopter parent. Give kids chores and responsibilities. Make them responsible for getting their homework done. Don't nag them, just make it an expectation. If not done, there should be a consequence. Nothing more, nothing less. Don't do everything for your children. Let them make mistakes and learn from them. We learn much more from mistakes than all the great things we do. Encourage lemonade stands, cotton candy stands or other types of businesses that kids can start during their summer breaks.

This teaches them many things including salesmanship and basic accounting. Encourage passions and skills whether it be sports, boy or girl scouts or computer coding skills. Have family time. Eat dinner together no matter how busy you are. Make them feel like they have a voice.

Anita Mahaffey, Cool-jams Inc

As a parent of super young kids, it's about ensuring that when the time comes to teach them about responsible online activity, they have that sense of ownership around their online presence and how they represent themselves. That 'ownership' is empowering and in the context of entrepreneurship says 'if you can be responsible for this, it means you can get out there and do your own thing!'

Melissa Schneider, GoDaddy

LEARNING LANGUAGES

JODIE

A sense of perspective is instrumental in entrepreneurship. Zooming out and seeing a situation from afar renders small details irrelevant and is an invaluable tool for evaluating what matters.

The sooner someone develops awareness of the world around them, the sooner they can practise perspective. Of the entrepreneurs and business leaders in my studies, many had some international experience in childhood. Examples included reading the international section of newspapers, being introduced to people from different cultures, or travelling themselves. They each became mindful that the way they lived wasn't the only way to live.

Options on where and how to live put the onlooker firmly in the driving seat of their own life. They won't accept how something is, because they know there's more available to them. If a child can see that there is more to life than their immediate surroundings, they can set their imagination to who they could become and what they could achieve.

In researching for this book, I interviewed twenty entrepreneurs, business owners and creatives for podcast episodes about the childhood influences that helped to create their future success (go to podcast.clevertykes.com). The stories were fascinating – we delved into dinner table conversations, childhood impressions of what work involves, as well as specific phrases their parents said to them as children that have stuck with them to this day.

As I interviewed more guests, I started to notice trends in their experiences. Many of the guests, for example, had moved home or school multiple times before they were age ten. They had been forced to adapt to a new city, school or friendship group and had each developed ways of doing this.

What tied nearly all of the guests together was that they had some form of worldly experience. Some of these included:

- Having a neighbour from a different country and talking to them about what their home country was like.

- Reading newspaper stories of events occurring all over the world.

- Having parents or relatives from different places and experiencing different cultures.

- Knowing of friends or family members who travelled a lot for work.

- Being taken to different parts of the world on holiday, although not all had that privilege.

- Spending time with school friends who spoke another language and learning it from them.

This meant that these people, from a young age, realised that there was a huge world out there waiting for them to explore. It helped them to think bigger than just their town or village or city. It helped them to consider the world from different perspectives and opened their eyes to possibilities. For raising entrepreneurial kids, this is a useful skill to develop.

Learning languages can make the world seem like a smaller place because you can now engage with more people. It helps you empathise. If you've ever tried talking to someone in their own language, you'll understand how hard it might be for someone to speak English.

Studies suggest that children learning an additional language tend to score better on standardised tests because learning languages develops listening, observation, problem-solving and critical thinking skills. These are transferable skills that are of life-long benefit, both personally and professionally.[37]

ACTIONABLES

- Decide together which language to learn. You could base your selection on your friendship group, any relatives for whom English isn't their first language, or an upcoming trip. This will mean you have people to practise with or a reason to practise.

- Obtain some sticky notes, look up translations and label objects around the house to learn nouns. We did this growing up and now I will never forget that 'fenster' means 'window' in German.

- Watch your favourite films with different language subtitles or dubbing. This is an option on most DVDs or online series.

- Use an app like Duolingo to learn together and test each other, as well as benchmark your progress.

- One Third Stories is a storybook series whose books start in one language and finish in another. Throughout the book, words are gradually replaced until the whole book is translated.

A scholarship to a local international college was all it took to get me hooked on global cultures, people and business. Attending Concord College in Shropshire in 1990 (showing my age!) was an incredible experience in being immersed in an environment I had not previously known. I was one of four British people in a college of a couple of hundred students from pretty much every corner of the globe. This encouraged me to add Japanese as a language when I went on to study law at university, which then led to a year spent in Japan, living with a home-stay family. Moving to a country that's far from home and having to adapt and thrive is an incredibly useful foundation for being your own boss as you need to quickly understand others' needs and figure out fast how to approach daily experiences to which you're not usually accustomed. In short, you have to get comfortable with getting out of your comfort zone! It was in Japan that I started my first business and I haven't turned my back on entrepreneurship since.

Emma Jones MBE, Enterprise Nation

I was born in the former Soviet Union (now Tbilisi, Georgia) and was raised under a communist regime. At an early age, my father encouraged me to learn English by watching C-SPAN (which was illegal at the time), which gave me a competitive advantage when I decided to move to the US. My parents also required that I read incessantly about immigrant business giants like Andrew Carnegie. I now view nothing as impossible, thinking of setbacks as hurdles that can be overcome.

George Arison, Shift

As a linguist, I have also taught my children Spanish and Italian. Being bilingual greatly benefits executive functioning which is critical to any entrepreneur. Languages will also help my children in whatever field they choose.

Caryn Antonini, Early Lingo, Inc

Learning languages is a big theme in my life. I was always fascinated with words and remember seeking connections between them when I was three or four years old. On holiday, my parents used to give me little tasks and teach me the necessary words to accomplish them, such as 'Une baguette, s'il vous plaît' to buy some bread at the French campsite. I believe this made me realise that you can achieve almost anything with language and that I'm able to adapt to new circumstances with the right information.

Sabine Harnau, From Scratch Communications

JACK MA

Known for: Founder of Alibaba

What else: An estimated net worth of $48.2 billion, and one of the wealthiest people in the world.[38]

Born in Hangzhou, located in the south-eastern part of China, from a young age Ma was keen on gathering knowledge about English and tried his best to communicate better in the language. After President Nixon visited Hangzhou in 1972, Ma's hometown became a tourist mecca and Jack wanted to make the most of this opportunity.

As a teenager, he started waking up early to visit the city's main hotel. For nine years, he rode the seventeen-mile journey to the hotel on his bicycle, giving tourists free tours of the area to practise his English. He became pen pals with one, who nicknamed him 'Jack' instead of pronouncing his real name. Ma aspired to go to university but had trouble being accepted onto a course. On his third attempt, he joined the Hangzhou Teacher's Institute to pursue a bachelor's degree in English.

He graduated in 1988 and then started applying to as many jobs as he could. He received more than a dozen rejections, including from KFC, before being hired as an English teacher. At the World Economic Forum in 2016, Jack Ma revealed he has been rejected from Harvard – ten times.[39] He founded Alibaba in 1999.

CODING

JODIE

Let's talk about screen time. In 2019 the World Health Organization (WHO) advised parents to limit screen time to just one hour a day for children under five.[40] Although Steve Jobs, Bill Gates and other Silicon Valley professionals raised their kids to be tech-free,[41] according to insiders, Silicon Valley professionals with Harvard MBAs are working continuously to create apps and websites that deliberately get us hooked.[42]

We can see the signs already. You might have noticed that kids scrolling through Netflix, YouTube or social media and playing on the Peppa Pig app isn't just a leisurely activity – it's often an addiction. There's a compulsion to do it and withdrawal might lead to tantrums, arguments and bargaining until the device is back or the screen is on.

The parents and educators we've discussed this with have various tactics to manage screen time, including:

- Planning regular activities outside.
- Limiting screens between certain hours, for example at mealtimes, in the evenings and first thing in the morning.
- Having gadget creches, where everyone's phone or iPad is stored between certain times.
- Opting out altogether.
- Limiting their own technology use in front of their kids to set an example.
- Installing a timer on the Wi-Fi router, keeping it locked away and limiting data limits on phone contracts.

A recent discussion, however, addressed how a parent could *mindfully* introduce technology to his children.

'I've been thinking about how to introduce screen and computer usage to my kids in a way that will set them up for success when they're older, without causing it to become a time suck, distraction or addiction. From what I'm seeing (and hearing from my older son's school), they have way less screen time than their peers. I'm happy about that, but I don't want to be so anti-screen that they fall behind.

'I'd like to eventually encourage them to learn how to use Google for "Just in Time Learning", how to build websites, how to code and how to have a relationship with AI and future tech. When should I be introducing them to computer usage? What does that look like? Googling? Building a WP website? Coding bootcamps? At what age is any of this appropriate?'

Curt Storring, parent, via a forum discussion on membership site Dynamite Circle

They're big questions. Mindlessly scrolling, playing games and becoming addicted to notifications isn't conducive to future success, for kids or adults. Producing – learning how to edit, code and create things of value – leads to building up invaluable skills and opening opportunities. Specifically introducing certain aspects is likely to prepare someone well for a working world where technology enables a business to go from serving a few to serving millions, perhaps with the same input.

ACTIONABLES

- Recording videos then editing them with iMovie.
  This could include 'show and tell' with toys, much like YouTubers
  do with new products; performances with siblings; or
  documentary-type videos about family trips, hobbies or interest
  areas.

- Setting up a SquareSpace or Shopify free trial to experiment with
  creating websites.

- Visiting www.kano.me or www.playpiper.com to introduce kids to
  learning to play with computers and code.

- Exploring how games are made instead of playing them.
  For example: www.code.org/minecraft

- Downloading the Daisy The Dinosaur app to teach the basics of
  coding in a fun way.

- Checking out coding courses where an instructor takes someone
  along a journey of learning how to perform basic coding
  functions before setting them to more complex projects.

- Reading about coding role models, including fictional character
  Code-it Cody, and real-life tech entrepreneurs like Mark
  Zuckerberg and Bill Gates.

When my daughter sees that something hasn't been offered to the
public, whether it be a 'how-to' or an app that hasn't been created,
I encourage her to create something, perhaps a YouTube video, so

that she taps into that entrepreneurial spirit. These are small things, but small habits lead to big changes. I'm hoping that as she grows, she'll spot opportunities to use her creativity and offer something to the public that's not already available. To that end, since I know she's very good with computers, I provided her with lessons for coding programs, which further her skills. By encouraging her to tap into her talents, skills and 'wants', she will hopefully feel compelled to originate ideas rather than simply be a follower.

Sarah Johnson, Fit Small Business

My parents still run a Taiwan-based manufacturing company in specialized adhesives. Growing up, our dinner conversations were around resolving personnel issues, which taught me human motivations at an early age. For hobbies, they motivated me to learn programming and music, as a way to stimulate creative thinking and technical aptitude.

Frank Lee, Bevi

When my son started asking about how to make a website after seeing me do some work on updating the site for my company, it was a chance to show him some fun and relatively easy web tools he could play around with. Soon enough, he and a friend had a rough web page and blog up and running! From there he and his buddy began brainstorming different products to sell via the website because, of course, that's what you do! Can't have a website without a business! I really feel that, because we jumped on that initial question and interest in websites, it opened up many avenues of learning and entrepreneurial encouragement. He started wanting to take coding classes so they could expand and upgrade their website, he was writing more because they needed content to update the blog, and there have been innumerable 'business meetings' with his friends as they work through what to sell on the site. They've also had many product development sessions trying different ingredients and tools to create their product, discussions on pricing, design, and on and on!

Mathew Burnett, Super Genius Inc

LARRY PAGE

Known for: Co-founder and former CEO of Google

What else: Co-inventor of PageRank, a well-known search ranking algorithm for Google, which he wrote with his Google co-founder Sergey Brin.

The child of a pair of computer science professors at Michigan State University, Page grew up in a messy house. There were computers, gadgets and tech magazines everywhere. The atmosphere – and Page's attentive parents – fostered creativity and invention. Page was an avid reader during his youth and spent a huge amount of time poring over books and magazines. At the age of twelve, he read the biography of Nikola Tesla, a great inventor who died penniless. Tesla's story taught him the first rudimental lesson on innovation: 'Invention is not enough. Tesla invented the electric power we use, but he struggled to get it out to people. You have to combine both things: invention and innovation focus, plus the company that can commercialise things and get them to people.'[43] This became his mission in life.

Page was first attracted to computers when he was six years old as he was able to play with the first-generation personal computers that had been left by his parents. He was the first in his elementary school to turn in an assignment from a word processor. His older brother also taught him to take things apart and before long he was taking everything in his house apart to see how it worked. He said that, 'I understood very early on that I wanted to invent things. So, I became really interested in technology and business. Probably from when I was twelve, I knew I was going to start a company eventually.'[44]

MAKING THINGS

JODIE

I was fascinated to interview Jordan Daykin for the podcast, who began a company with his grandad in 2008 when Jordan was just thirteen. Jordan's net worth is now over £18 million. Jordan's parents split up when he was nine years old, and he went to live with his grandparents because his father was moving to Sierra Leone for work.

Jordan's grandad, an engineer, was helping him move into the garage, which they had decided to convert into a bedroom. During the conversion, Jordan was trying to hang a blackout blind and a curtain rail. In doing this, Jordan and his grandad broke several fixings and drill bits. The two went to their local hardware store to find a solution, but found nothing.

Jordan recalls seeing his grandad making things at work throughout his childhood. He would take things apart to put them back together and was always intently interested in how something worked – how this cog turned this wheel, and so on. When Jordan and his grandad couldn't find what they were looking for, they decided to make it for themselves. The result was a wall-fixing invention named GripIt, that went on to successfully wall-mount a TV. It was patented and eventually sold in thirty-two countries.

Not every homemade invention will go on to be a worldwide commercial success, but you never know what can be created. The most valuable learning points from most home-making efforts will be:

- Seeing inputs directly lead to outputs. Whether that's baking or making art or objects, the ingredients and raw materials combine to create something with a function greater than those raw materials alone.

- Experimenting, playing and seeing what happens. Learning how things work and how they don't work fires synapses which lead to understanding and remembering.

🚀 Risk-free trying. You could stumble upon an invention that changes the world for millions; you could just create something that looks nice. Either way, it's a game and there's no pressure.

ACTIONABLES

In practice, this could involve:

🚀 Using toys and games like Lego and Duplo where there isn't necessarily a right or wrong answer – the focus is on experimenting and creativity.

🚀 Using toys and games like jigsaws or puzzles, where there is a right answer and it takes creativity and perseverance to get there.

🚀 Asking, 'What else could you do with this?' about different everyday items.

🚀 Setting out the raw materials and not being prescriptive about what is created. Make something useful, make something pretty or just make a mess.

My dad could build, design and fix anything; but instead of just doing it for me, he would make sure I was part of the process, teaching me each step of the way. In the end, I not only understood the process, but could do it on my own. The encouragement to go out on a limb and the understanding of any process or procedure are skills that stick with me to this day and have helped me in my journey as an entrepreneur.

Kirsten Potenza, POUND Rockout Workout

In our house, actual making is a big thing. We typically collect cardboard boxes and other materials for my nine-year-old to just build or enact her ideas. This allows her to go into sponge mode, asking questions such as, 'How can I do this?' Figuring it out on her own also gives her the permission to not have to know everything, but teaches the value of exploration, cultivating a beginner's mindset and curiosity while fostering persistence. Instead of buying a shelter for stuffed animals; build one. Instead of buying dress-up clothes; make some. Creating a sweet shop? Just do it. It empowers her to think through the creation process and when constructions or products fail, to iterate and do it over again, with each failure gaining more answers. We also heavily embrace boredom and my standard response to, 'Mama, I am so bored' is typically, 'Good, enjoy! That's when you are starting to get really creative.'

Monique Fuchs, Accelerate Center

Once a shy young girl with anxiety, my transformation into a confident attorney and, subsequently, entrepreneur was in no small part because of the lessons I learned from my parents. When I was in elementary school, we were assigned to create a diorama of a Spanish Mission. As I walked through the aisles of the art store, I was immediately drawn to a diorama kit. As I reached for it, my mother said, 'No way! That is cheating.' She then guided me to the other sections of the store and made me figure out how I would make each part from scratch. After weeks of diligently making each wall, each bell, each tree, each everything by hand, I looked at what I had created with pride. When the day came to reveal all of my hard work at school, I was initially a little ashamed as my jagged walls and imperfect bells stood next to the beautiful store-bought kits. That is until the teacher ran over and exclaimed, 'Look at this! The creativity, the attention to detail. This is one of my favorites. This is what I wanted to see.' Since then, I have never feared starting from scratch.

Brittany Merrill Yeng, Skrewball Peanut Butter Whiskey

SELLING

JODIE

It was 2011. I had just launched my social media agency and I was about to attend my first ever meeting with a potential client. My dad has managed car dealerships for much of his career, so I asked him for advice on selling. He told me this:

1. Knowledge instils confidence.

2. Confidence instils enthusiasm.

3. Enthusiasm sells cars and vans.

It didn't matter that I was selling social media management and not cars and vans, the sentiment still applied. I decided that what I lacked in experience I would make up for in knowledge, so I extensively researched the company I was going to see. I read all the information about them online, I found their team members on LinkedIn, I understood their purpose and vision and what they did. As I was researching, I found myself getting so many ideas of what I could do for them. Ideas for articles popped into my head, as did thoughts on whom I could approach on their behalf using Twitter and the kind of content I could create for them. I made a list of questions I wanted to ask, and conversation starters to use based on what I'd read about the previous roles of the founders. Before I knew it, I felt prepared and excited for the meeting.

I was eager to arrive, meet the founders and share my ideas. During the meeting, I could confidently explain what I'd seen and what I thought I could do that would add value. It didn't matter that I'd never done it before because the knowledge had instilled confidence, the confidence had instilled enthusiasm. The founders bought into it and were happy to let me execute the ideas I had proposed. Win. To this day, they don't know that they were my first client or that our meeting was my first prospect meeting.

After I won my first client, I gained experience, and I was certain that my 'knowledge, confidence, enthusiasm' process was the right one. Experience then led to sale two, and three and four...

If you look at how salespeople are portrayed in TV shows and films (think Harry Wormwood – Matilda's dad) or you type 'salesperson' into a stock image site, the picture you're most likely to see is someone with the gift of the gab who is able to convince innocent people to part with their cash in exchange for something that's not very good. But in real life, it's not like that.

In its simplest form, making a sale involves understanding someone's needs and being able to provide a solution. For the solution to be relevant, the seller has to understand the needs of the buyer. For the buyer to buy, the seller has to sufficiently show that their solution is the one the buyer should choose.

I remember my dad teaching me persuasion techniques in jest. He'd say, 'Do you want to tidy your room?' while nodding furiously, as if to imply what the correct answer was. He also taught me what he called dual positive questions in jest, like, 'Do you want to tidy your room or hoover your sister's?', failing to mention option three, which was to do neither.

ACTIONABLES

Here are some ideas to prepare someone for making sales, which include developing skills in empathy and persuasion:

Empathy

Practise seeing something from someone else's point of view. This could include people you meet in your day-to-day, friends and siblings or even characters in television shows or books. Questions can include:

- What's their side of the story?

- Why do you think they did that?

- What do they want?

- Why did person A say that?

- Why did person B respond like that?

Persuasion

Practise framing something as an opportunity for someone else and make reasonable requests that are more likely to be well received. When asking something of someone, think, 'What's in it for them?' Practise this in everyday interactions with others, for example:

- When they want to borrow something, when they want to join in a game or when they want to go somewhere.

- When asking for a lift somewhere ('It's your chance to visit x place on the way back').

- When asking to borrow something ('I'll bring it back cleaner than before').

- When asking for a favour ('I'll repay you next week by doing x').

There are times that we don't even realize the seeds our parents are planting in us until years later. I remember riding around my grandparents' neighborhood in New Jersey when I was a kid, and my mother telling me stories of the candy store my grandfather used to own when she was a kid. Somehow hearing those stories led me to set up my own candy store in my grandparents' living room. At the time, my 'store' consisted of separating a bag of Skittles by color, putting them into individual cups and selling the Skittles for 5 cents each. My parents and grandparents never complained about my exorbitant prices or mark-up (they were my only customers) and visited my 'store' each time I was there for a visit. I'm grateful for that small seed being planted so many years ago, celebrating my ideas and encouraging me as a budding entrepreneur.

Shannon Simpson Jones, Verb

I didn't get pocket money as I misbehaved at school and home (ADHD) so I had to make my own money. At about age seven to eight I was washing cars and mowing lawns. By the age of ten I bought bankrupt stock and sold it door-to-door, making £500 profit. At twelve I was selling mix tapes at school to buy my first DJ decks. I also used to go to the Leeds United ground every morning in the holidays and auction off signed shirts in the free-ads newspaper. I'm not actually sure who spurred me to become entrepreneurial, as none of my family were or are business owners.

Danny Savage, dannysavage.com

I learned how to sell things early on. My parents sent me to flea markets from an early age. I sold whatever we found in our basement or old toys, gadgets, etc I didn't need or want any longer. I was always doing the selling and negotiating with buyers. I must have been no older than maybe seven years old when I went to my first flea market and then went to several the following years, not because we 'needed' the money but because my parents felt like learning how to sell things must have been important.

Chris Erhardt, Tunedly

NEGOTIATING

JODIE

There's a difference between a negotiation and an argument. An argument usually concerns conflicting opinions or beliefs and in an argument there is a winner and a loser.

A negotiation might involve conflicting goals or interests, but a solution can be reached involving both parties compromising to achieve the best combined result. In a negotiation, if done well, there are no winners and losers – there are only winners. Negotiations don't need to be zero-sum games as long as each party is open and willing to work to a solution.

Sometimes the best way to negotiate is to avoid a negotiation altogether.

In Ichiro Kishimi's book *The Courage to Be Disliked*,[45] he talks about the separation of tasks based on Adlerian psychology. The premise of this is that 'you focus on your tasks and I'll focus on mine'. The beliefs or opinions that someone holds are their concern. You don't need to be concerned with them until they directly affect you.

The first questions are, 'Does this need to be an argument? Can we agree to disagree and each focus on our own tasks independently of each other?'

Within a home or school setting, sometimes negotiation is inevitable. For a successful negotiation, each party needs to understand the wants and needs of the other to propose a solution they will both accept and reach a compromise.

ACTIONABLES

There are three distinct components to negotiating, each of which can be practised and modelled in day-to-day scenarios.

1. Active listening and ascertaining when you're in a negotiation:

   Highlight when you're in a negotiation with your child or when they're in one with a sibling. Equally, highlight when you are not in a negotiation. Learn negotiation techniques yourself, to model them. A good book for this is *Getting to Yes: Negotiating agreement without giving in* by Roger Fisher and William Ury.[46]

2. Problem-solving: setting out the terms of the negotiation:

   Identify what the 'non-negotiables' of a deal are and create a priority list. Ask, 'What else can you offer me?' in order that they think more broadly. Ask, 'What's really important to you here?' and encourage them to do the same.

3. Speaking effectively and concisely, showing assertiveness without aggression:

   Play 'the orange game' where two groups negotiate to own an orange based on their own needs and understanding the needs of the other party.[47] Practise time-outs. If a negotiation is getting heated, they can say, 'I need a time-out' and take five minutes to think and regain composure.

Market stalls and car boot sales are good places to hone negotiation skills in a safe environment.

I have taught them about bargain shopping and how not to pay full price, especially when it comes to retail where the mark-up is big. My kids also understand that shopping around and negotiating is key, especially when it comes to cable contracts, phone vendor contracts and other things they care about like gadgets, electronics, shoes, etc.

Jackie Rednour-Bruckman, MyWorkDrive

When I was growing up, my parents and grandparents would take my siblings and me to flea markets. On a somewhat rare occasion, my grandfather would purchase things for one of us. And when he did, he and my parents had an agreement: if I wanted something that was just a little pricier than necessary, I had to negotiate with the vendor and purchase it myself from the money he gave me. This taught me two lessons. First, if I wanted something, I'd have to advocate for myself. Second, some things are negotiable, and negotiation isn't the worst form of human interaction. The latter lesson has been invaluable to me as an entrepreneur because I don't personally like the conflict that negotiation often creates. But because of that childhood training of negotiation with adults for my own toys or books at flea markets, I'm much more comfortable with negotiating than most people I encounter.

Kreigh Knerr, Knerr Learning Center

My father taught me that it doesn't hurt to ask; the worst is that people will say no. I remember this when I am asking for a discount with a vendor, or help with understanding how a product or service works. Asking good questions encourages other people to want to see you be successful. My father treated me with respect and asked me for my input even at a young age, he never made feel dumb if I didn't know the answer, I felt like he treated me like his strategy partner and therefore the process made me try harder.

Shirley Tan, PostureKeeper

GARY VAYNERCHUK

Known for: Founder of VaynerMedia and VaynerX

What else: Gary transformed his family's wine business from a $3m to a $60m valuation business within a few years.

After spending the first three years of his life in Babruysk in Belarus, Vaynerchuk moved to the US with his family. In a live Q&A session, he talks about how his mum raised him. 'When I was nine years old and I opened the door for an elderly woman at McDonald's she acted like I'd won the Nobel Peace Prize. What my mum did was super smart. She overreacted on everything that I was doing that was a good human trait and she held me accountable for things that didn't matter, like grades... My mum built huge self-esteem in me and I feel like the biggest reason I am who I am today to everybody is because I feel so guilty and grateful for what she did for me that I want to do it for everybody else.'[48]

My mother taught me how to believe in myself the most, while still allowing me to recognise the value in others ... She downplayed the things that she knew didn't matter as much for me (like school) while also teaching me to respect them at the same time (ie, I couldn't run wild in school or curse my teachers) ... She gave me the perfect mix of freedom, support, acknowledgement and, most importantly, was able to see my strengths and encouraged me to play to them.'[49]

PITCHING

JODIE

Children have transient wants and needs. Asking them to pitch for something helps them think through if they actually want it and teaches skills that will be valuable to them in their later lives and careers.

HEY COME OUTSIDE
AND LET'S DO SOME
REAL PITCHING

Helping children understand the concept of a pitch will build a foundation for them to do it well:

- 🚀 The *reason* someone is pitching in the first place is that they want to achieve something – an action or decision that will benefit them.

- 🚀 The *purpose* of a pitch is to help everyone in the room come to the conclusion that taking the action or decision is in the best interests of more than just the person pitching. Work on the basis that everyone in the room has a different view of the world and that they may see problems with your idea. Everyone will be balancing pros and cons from their viewpoint.

- 🚀 There is a structure for a perfect pitch:

1. Provide a summary of the request.

2. Outline the problem that needs solving.

3. Say why your proposed solution is the right one (pros).

4. Give consideration to the challenges and objections (cons or perceived cons).

5. Give your audience time for questions and answers.

6. Provide a conclusion before the final decision making.

ACTIONABLES

There are a number of ways to develop the practice of preparing pitches using the structure provided above:

- Give them the option of introducing pitch documents, which could be physical handouts or, more likely, slides in a PowerPoint presentation. Help them add headings to pages and then guide them on what they could put under each one.

- Keep asking questions and encourage them to include the answers in their pitch.

- Depending on the age of your children, watching specific pitches from *Dragons' Den* might help bring pitching to life.

- Take it seriously. Set a time for the pitch, turn off other distractions and give it your full attention. It also teaches public speaking skills and helps overcome shyness.

- Repeat the exercise more than once so that they experience being successful and unsuccessful.

- Pitch for fun. Getting a pet, choosing a certain meal for dinner or starting a new hobby can all be pitches.

When I was fifteen, I wanted to try internet affiliate marketing, which required a seed investment of around $600 to get a website up and running. I didn't have that kind of money, so I pitched my parents on what I was looking to do, why I thought it would work, and how I was going to make money on the project. I'm sure the vast majority of parents would have thought the whole idea was ridiculous, but my parents decided to lend me the money and chalk it up to a learning experience if I failed. That $600 investment lead to a six-figure sale of the business a few years later, which provided me with the seed capital to launch my current company, JM Bullion.

Michael Wittmeyer, JM Bullion, Inc

Both of my daughters are good pitchers! They know to come to me with complete information and the benefits of the pitch if they want something that's outside of the norm. For example, recently my daughter wanted a new microscope that was more expensive than necessary for her class. She showed me a number of competitively priced brands and explained how it would help her and be a good investment because she would need a better one in a couple of years. I agreed and she got a better-quality microscope.

Laura Hunter, LashLiner LLC

I'm the fourth-generation owner of a commercial construction company based in St. Louis, so I grew up learning about our family's business – accompanying my father to job sites, discussing business at the dinner table, hauling materials in high school, and picking up bits of information along the way. For as long as I can remember, my father asked me to negotiate or make a pitch for what I wanted, and now I'm having my daughters do the same thing. Growing up, when I asked my parents for something – anything from staying out late to going on a trip with my buddies for spring break – I got the same response: 'Come back when you have all of the information.' I would return with a prepared pitch, and I was rewarded for a persuasive argument or a fair negotiation.

For example, when I asked to stay out past curfew, I gave my father all of the information I had – who I would be with, where I would be, how often I would check in, etc – along with my reasoning. Sometimes it worked, sometimes it didn't, but now I'm teaching those same skills to my kids. Last month, my ten-year-old daughter asked for her first phone, and I told her she needed to create a presentation. I gave her a few hints on topics to include (Eg, how much does a phone cost? How will you earn money to pay for it? How will you use it responsibly?) but mostly she was encouraged to make her pitch. She ended up designing a full deck on Google Drive (which she can access through her school district) complete with sourced research, graphics and colorful fonts. As a small business owner, everything I do involves pitching or negotiating, so I'm working hard to pass those skills on to my kids.

Tim Spiegelglass, Spiegelglass Construction Company

THE NEEDS OF OTHERS

There's a bias that can happen when individuals assess their own and others' behaviour: attribution bias.[50] When judging others, we tend to assume their actions are the result of internal factors such as their personality, whereas we tend to assume our own actions arise because of the necessity of external circumstances.

When someone turns up late to a meeting, you might label them as lazy or inconsiderate, but they will explain their lateness by pointing to the traffic jam or the person they helped with directions on the way to meet you. It is paramount to understand the actions of others and not judge or label them as a bad person.

In schools, this might be taught as character education. 'Character education'[51] involves teaching children in ways that will ensure they act in a moral, virtuous, good-mannered and non-bullying manner. A key part of character education is thinking about the needs of others, a perfect trait for future entrepreneurs.

Empathy is a skill. As humans, we are generally programmed to put our own wants and needs first. Appreciating the needs of others is hugely beneficial in the world of entrepreneurship. Most businesses rely on their customers' needs, as these contribute to the demand for their products or services. Without a business understanding the needs of its customers, being successful will be difficult.

Understanding someone's motivators for buying or doing anything gives you an advantage in making a deal, designing a product or pitching a new idea. There are ways to practise this early on, so it soon becomes second nature.

ACTIONABLES

- Share stories of empathy. Talk about people who have considered the needs of others as role models.

- Talk about characters in books together. Understand their personalities, what they like and don't like and the attributes they show. Pick peripheral characters, not just the main protagonist.

- When they are upset with something someone else did, focus on understanding why the other person did that.

- A compliment a day. Give compliments and encourage your kid to give them to others, when appropriate.

- Before they carry out an action that affects someone else, ask 'How might x feel?' Siblings are good examples because they can be the hardest people to empathise with.

- Practise noticing people. For everyone you pass, ask, 'What are they here to do? What do they need?'

- People watch. Find a park bench or somewhere to sit in the city. Pick people who pass by and create their stories. What do they like? What makes them happy? What problems are they trying to solve? How could you help them?

- Exaggerate for fun. If you're making tea or coffee for guests, ask your kid to quiz each guest on how they would like their drink, and keep quizzing them until you know how much milk they would like to the nearest millimetre and how much sugar to the nearest gram. Exaggerate making someone's perfect drink just how they like it.

- Practise random acts of kindness. Talk together about the random acts you could carry out and for whom.

Each day, a little time [with my five-year-old daughter] is spent talking about relationships – grandparents, classmates, friends, characters in stories or even individuals in our lives that our daughter interacts with. We talk about what she has seen go well, what she has heard, what she saw go poorly and then we look at why that situation went that way. Did it help the relationship? What would she do differently to better build the relationship or avoid the challenges it created? From this, she grows stronger in building her own direct relationships and understanding those between others each day. I have found that strong relationship management is a core foundation in entrepreneurship – be it with clients, team members or competitors. In every case, it is always better to know the individuals, understand them and be equipped to manage every interaction appropriately.

Mark Concannon, Concannon Business Consulting

My parents taught me at a young age to do something you love, and something that makes a difference in people's lives. They each were taught the same thing, and that led them to be business owners themselves. This simple motto always stuck with me.

If you wake up each day and don't enjoy what you are doing and don't see the impact of what you do for others, chances are you'll get burned out of whatever field you are in. Having this type of mentality generally will separate you from your competition.

Matt Schmidt, Diabetes Life Solutions

I often use the 'duvet on a cold night' analogy for this one. A tug of the duvet to the left leaves the person to the right feeling chilly and the reverse is just the same. We encourage our daughter to always seek to understand the wider impacts of her actions and in particular how this might affect the feelings of others and ultimately to act in favour of the greater good. For now, we teach this mostly through encouraging 'good play' during playdates with her peers, and how to self-conflict resolve when inevitably one toddler wants an extra turn on the playground slides. Empathy and being open to the views of others are important values for us as parents. We appreciate that given the singularity of our life experiences, it is difficult to single-handedly devise the best solutions, therefore we must seek out diversity of thought by collaborating and working with people of different backgrounds. Although the teaching opportunity for this life lesson does not yet present itself (she is only three years old) we welcome the opportunity to expand on it as she grows older.

Kathryn Campbell, Google

AMANCIO ORTEGA

Known for: Founder of Inditex group, parent brand of ZARA

What else: Known to be a down-to-earth man who stays away from the media and has rarely granted interviews.

Ortega was born at the beginning of the Civil War in a small village in Spain with fewer than 100 citizens. He was the youngest of four children. Ortega's father had a job at the local railway station, and the family lived onsite in the workers' quarters. The family was extremely poor and Ortega remembered experiencing his mother pleading with local stores to grant them credit on essential items.

Inspired to change his trajectory and have a different life, Ortega left school and started working as a shop assistant when he was fourteen. Here, he learned to make clothes by hand and realised that earning decent money involved nothing more than giving customers what they want.

In 1975, Ortega opened his first store in the same city. It was named Zorba, after his and his first wife's favourite movie. Later, the store name was changed to ZARA. The brand values hold true to the lessons Ortega learned when working his first role: give customers what they want, as quickly as possible.[52]

PART 3
ENTREPRENEURIAL OPPORTUNITIES

DANIEL

At age ten my father picked me up from karate practice with a solemn face. He explained that there had been a small fire in the house while I was out and the house was full of smoke and soot. Some hot oil had ignited the curtains, the curtains had set fire to the wall and the cupboards, and a big hole had been burned in the kitchen before the blaze had been extinguished. Fortunately, no one was hurt.

The following day, everything that had been damaged by smoke was piled up into the trailer ready to be taken to the tip. It was at this point I had a brainwave: What if I clean this stuff and sell it rather than throwing it away? My mother encouraged the idea and I was given a week to make good on the venture or else everything would be taken to the tip.

I cleaned the items diligently; organised a poster for the local corner store window; and put a classified ad in the paper marketing my garage sale. The night before the sale I realised that I didn't have all that much stock and there was plenty of room for more goods to be sold. I went to the neighbours and agreed a 50/50 joint venture on any of the goods I could sell on their behalf.

The following morning, dozens of people showed up and purchased most of the goods. The high point was when one customer asked to speak to my dad so he could negotiate the price of the smoke-blackened microwave. My father responded with, 'It's his business, not mine. You will have to negotiate with Daniel.' I felt a huge sense of empowerment and at the end of the day I had made a cool $300 (AUD) – enough to buy a BMX bike and a SEGA Master System.

Giving your kids an opportunity to succeed or fail in real life is a wonderful gift. Learning from experiences is how people learn best. Experimenting with skills and ideas on a small scale is a critical step towards bigger things.

As the founder of a business accelerator, I talk to hundreds of entrepreneurs each year about their ambitions. One of the biggest barriers to success for many people is a lack of confidence. It's not uncommon to hear a fifty-year-old man tell me that he's nervous and lacks confidence to go after his dreams despite the logical arguments stacking up.

Confidence is linked to familiarity. A little bravado can be helpful to get started, but the way we get really confident at something is through experience. Giving a talk in front of a group of people can be nerve-wracking the first time you do it, but if you do it every week you soon find yourself completely comfortable speaking to a room full of strangers.

The sooner a person starts this process of stepping out of their familiar comfort zone to seize an opportunity, the more natural it will become. When it comes to raising entrepreneurial kids, what you view as small tasks can often be big opportunities for your children.

As a child, when Jodie was given the responsibility of packing her own suitcase to go on holiday it would have only taken her mother a few minutes to pack for her but the opportunity to perform this important activity would have been lost. Instead, Jodie felt a sense of responsibility, autonomy and potential for failure. This was a building block of confidence for the future.

At a slightly older age, she was tasked with the responsibility of booking her own doctor's appointment. She had to look up the number, call the clinic and speak to the receptionist. An effortless task for an adult became another exciting opportunity for her to engage with the big, wide world and ultimately chalk up another win.

These building blocks of confidence add up. By the time Jodie was twenty-two, she was confidently calling up an accountant and starting her own company. She launched a new service and signed up dozens of clients. Each step outside of a person's comfort zone feels huge to them. Whether it's booking a doctor's appointment or launching a business, the feelings are the same. Giving your kids a chance to experience those feelings and then to rise above them is essential for success in life.

What happens if they fail? What happens if you give your little one an opportunity and they blow it? Well that is part of life too – not everything goes to plan and that's OK.

A friend of mine, Jeremy Harbour, was encouraged by his parents to sell some goods at car boot sales when he was thirteen. By fifteen he was buying wholesale jewellery and selling it for a significant mark-up at a local market stall on the weekends. He dropped out of school to grow his business and by age eighteen he had built up a steady income. He then put everything he had into a new arcade game venture he was sure would take off. Unfortunately, he misjudged the market and his business flopped.

Jeremy's unpaid bills stacked up quickly and before the age of twenty he found himself facing insolvency. He sent off the letters to his creditors, notifying them that his business was bankrupt and waited for the responses. He felt so scared of the consequences he couldn't get out of bed for days or bring himself to check his phone or open his mail – how could he face the world as a failure? Finally, he plucked up the courage to face the day and when he ventured outside, he discovered that nothing much had changed. He was the same person, except he no longer had the stress of the bills. There were no nasty letters, no ranting voice messages and no irate suppliers camped outside his door.

Jeremy discovered a valuable lesson. 'It felt like I was walking on a tightrope but when I fell off, I discovered that I was only six inches off the ground.' Facing failure so young gave Jeremy a unique view on life and business and a healthy tolerance for risk. Today, he's a multi-millionaire with a happy family, houses around the world, a luxury powerboat and a private jet. He says unequivocally that the experience of failure early on was a big key to his success later on.

Many parents and guardians think that they have to find grandiose opportunities for their kids. They think they have to get them a job placement with a dynamic start-up or make sure they develop coding skills that would rival Mark Zuckerberg. Your kids don't need huge opportunities to hone their skills; often it's simple and easy opportunities to do something a little bit outside their comfort zone.

In this section, you will see simple things like taking your kids to work can make a big impact. Letting your teens set up or manage a social media account for your business can be a massive responsibility that shows them they are trusted. You will see that the local neighbourhood is awash with entrepreneurial opportunities and many successful business owners did jobs for their neighbours as teens.

Children want opportunities to try new things and constantly ask for them. One parent we spoke to discovered something interesting about the ingenuity of his teenage son. Rather than paying his son an hourly rate to clean the pool each weekend, he paid him £10 per week for the pool to be *kept clean*. This slight change caused something interesting to happen: the older son outsourced some of the easier work to his younger brother for £3 per week and the two of them found quick and efficient ways to keep the pool clean all the time. What started as an opportunity to complete chores spiralled into an opportunity to form a team and innovate.

I will never forget the look on the face of the man at my garage sale when he was told it was my business and he would have to negotiate with me. I stuck to my guns and he paid my price for the microwave oven. In that moment I received a lot more than the money – the opportunity was priceless.

Chores could be negotiated based on the value we were able to bring to the table for a task. Instead of finite tasks, my parents encouraged me to submit ideas of how I could make extra money and if it would be useful to them, they would let me know what they could offer. I love this model and plan to use it with my own kids. I think it helps break people out of the standard nine to five job mentality.

Casey Hill, Hill Gaming Company

I have hired my daughter for many projects but I don't pay her by the hour. I have always paid her based on performance. The more she gets done the more she makes.

Doug Mitchell, Ogletree Financial

I have taught my kids what income, gross profit, net income, profit margin, and expenses mean so that they have a pretty good understanding of a basic [profit and loss] P&L statement. You want to make and sell cupcakes for money? What's your cost of goods and what's the cost of your labor? Subtract those totals and you have profit. Scaling that to something bigger is easy once you have the fundamentals. Also, teaching them to think of things or how to do things that make more profit without increasing labor and expenses is the key. For example, you could ask the neighbors if they need help raking their leaves or walking their dog but why not learn how to make paracord bracelets and pump a lot of them out in one hour and sell each one for $5/piece? You can make a lot more money in sales from one hour of labor rather than working harder all day and making less.

Jackie Rednour-Bruckman, MyWorkDrive

DECISION MAKING

JODIE

In 2010 I enrolled on a year-long graduate scheme with the National Skills Academy for Social Care. During the year I had the opportunity for regular coaching sessions. My assigned coach was Joanne Rule MBE and she had worked extensively in transformational healthcare before becoming a business coach.

Joanne worked with me on overcoming obstacles and creating a plan for what I would do after my graduate scheme came to an end. She became an accountability partner and gave me a framework for decision making that I still use today.

Imagine I had arrived at my coaching session with a specific challenge that I wanted to get past. The first thing Joanne and I would talk through was the challenge itself. What exactly was it? Why had it presented itself? Was it stand-alone or was it linked to other challenges? Why did it feel uncomfortable? What was the exact question we were trying to answer?

We'd dissect the challenge thoroughly before turning to the second step: deciding what to do about it. We would write the challenge down in the middle of a piece of paper. Then Joanne would simply ask, 'What could you do?' I would give an answer. No explanation of *why* was required at this point, just a short description of one possible option. Then she would ask, 'What else could you do?' and I'd give another answer. This would repeat until I was stuck for other possible answers. One answer that we always wrote down was, 'Do nothing'. Do nothing is always an option. Then, even when my mind was blank and I was sure I could think of no other possible solutions, Joanne would say, 'What else could you do?' and wait patiently while I searched my brain to give another answer. She never filled the silence created by my thinking and she never attempted to give answers for me – she just waited and let me find them.

Next, we were on to step three: elimination of answers. This involved analysing and crossing off the potential solutions, starting from the worst idea, answering the question, 'What might happen if you did that?' until there were only one or two options remaining to analyse and decide upon.

The spider diagram framework we used is based on three questions:

1. What is the problem?

2. What (else) could you do?

3. What might happen if you did that?

The key is that they were questions that I had to answer. My coach didn't jump to problem-solve for me or suggest answers for me. She was confident that I had the solutions myself; I just had to think hard enough to see them.

Not only did I reach the solution that I was most comfortable with, I was even more confident in it because I had eliminated the other options, plus I had thought of it myself. I wonder if I'd have been as motivated to progress with the solution if it had been someone else's idea.

As a parent or employer, it's so easy to jump into problem-solving mode and start coming up with ideas for what someone could do next. In the short term it requires patience, but it's far more beneficial in the long term if the people in our care trust in their own ability to find the answer and use a decision making framework to get there. I now use the spider diagram framework to make most of my decisions. I wrote everything out on paper at first but soon I no longer needed to.

I know that if I'd have practised spider diagrams and deliberate decision making from a younger age, I might not have made some of the career or education choices I did. Perhaps you feel the same. It's easy to follow the default path without questioning it.

In the future, young people will be presented with all sorts of opportunities that they need to assess. Continuing education, starting a job, applying to college or university, joining a start-up. Whatever it is, having a robust framework for decision making means these decisions will be made intentionally and deliberately, for the best possible outcome.

ACTIONABLES

Find an opportunity to use the three-step methodology described above:

- Make it fun. Use big sheets of paper and brightly coloured pens for your spider diagrams.
- Carry out the exercise for small and big decisions alike, to embed the skill.

I often challenge my kids with problem-solving to encourage their creative thinking, sharing a simple task from my own business and asking them how they'd approach it, or asking for their advice on a recipe or flavour, and encouraging them to be specific with their feedback so they understand the difference between opinion and actionable insight. I'm always blown away by the conversations, and they love knowing that the challenges are real, and that they're helping in some way. I like to think of it as a role play for the creative thinkers of the future, and I always learn something too!

Amy Cheadle, The Northern Dough Co

My parents taught me that, first, you have to believe in yourself. Second you have to think ten years in advance. You need to visualize where you want to be. Once you know, you must take the lead on to how to get there. Once you find the opportunity, you must take it head-on and jump in like you are diving into a pool. Once you get there, you have no choice but to swim. Even if you make a mistake, it will just teach you how to be better. The most important thing is to do the first step, then the second step and once you arrive at the third step you are already used to it.

Igal Dahan, Igal Dahan Jewelry

The thing I remember the most from my childhood is something that my mother taught me that still influences all of my decisions today. I was always an ambitious child, but I would be terrified of anything not working out. I'd talk about the hundreds of ways something could go wrong and I'd plan for the worst every time. My mother, no matter the situation, would always say, 'You'll figure it out.' When anything bad happened in our family, she'd say, 'We'll figure it out.' It was her go-to response for everything – when I didn't get the grade I wanted, or make the team I wanted, when I didn't get into the college I wanted to go to, when a relationship ended – when anything happened in my life, I'd find her and tell her and she'd say, 'It'll be ok because you'll figure it out.'

Now as an entrepreneur (and in my personal life), I find myself less afraid of failure, more willing to take risks, and more content with change than my colleagues and friends. I go into every decision with the mindset that no matter what happens, I'll figure it out. I believe that this one phrase my mother continued to use has influenced every decision I've ever made, and taught me not to worry about things that are out of my control.

Hayley Luckadoo, Luckadoo Media Co.

MARK ZUCKERBERG

Known for: Founder of Facebook
What else: *TIME* magazine's Person
of the Year 2010.

Growing up as one of four children, Mark's father, Edward Zuckerberg, ran a dental practice attached to the family's home. His mother, Karen, worked as a psychiatrist.

Zuckerberg developed an interest in computers at elementary school and, at the age of ten, discovered that the world was split into programmers and users. He was taught how to program by his father and when he was twelve he used Atari BASIC to create a messaging program he named ZuckNet. His father used the program in his dental office so that the receptionist could inform him of a new patient without yelling across the room. The family also used ZuckNet to communicate within the house.

Together with his friends, he also created computer games just for fun. 'I had a bunch of friends who were artists,' he said. 'They'd come over, draw stuff, and I'd build a game out of it.'[53]

In a radio interview with Edward Zuckerberg, he talks about some rules he followed when raising his family that led to their entrepreneurial behaviour:

1. Model working for yourself.

2. Provide security for them.

3. Discover and encourage their interests.

4. Show them you're proud of them.

5. Set limits and enforce them.

6. Make sure they play, too.[54]

STRATEGY

JODIE

Growing up there was a computer game called Theme Park World that I loved. It involved being the manager of my own virtual theme park. In the game I used a seed sum of virtual money to design and build the rides and open the park to customers, then I was responsible for making the park profitable. To make this happen I had to make decisions on ticket pricing, location of food stalls, where to build toilets and bins as well as hiring and training staff to maintain the park.

The success of the theme park I built was also measured by the happiness of attendees. If the park wasn't clean and tidy, customers were unhappy. If rides broke down and I hadn't hired enough engineers to fix them, customers were unhappy. If the queues for the food stalls were too long or the food was too expensive, customers were unhappy. This had a knock-on effect of selling fewer park tickets and not being able to build new rollercoasters.

I used to spend hours on the game. I tested different scenarios, experimenting with hiring magicians to entertain people waiting in line, or hiring more cleaners to clear away litter, to holding weekday ticket sales to level demand for the park. It was an incredible way to experiment with running a business. Even when I wasn't playing the game, my mind was whirring with solutions for how to fix problems and make the park a success – much like having a real business.

The two main benefits of playing this game were:

1.   Long-term planning

For every action I took or change I made, the reaction was realised minutes, hours or days down the line in my virtual world. I had to be good at predicting the future and planning for every eventuality. I had to run this theme park so it would be profitable in the long term, not just that day.

2. Assessing different scenarios

Every move also involved a cost-benefit analysis, and often some quick maths. If I increase ticket prices by 5% will customers spend 5% less on food and be 10% less likely to return? If the park is clean and tidy can I open and maintain fewer food stalls because customers will enjoy walking around? How much does the layout of the park affect how long people stay and how long they have to wait in lines?

Looking back, the transferable skills were clear. All of these skills are relevant to the daily life of an entrepreneur, even if my business isn't a theme park.

ACTIONABLES

Similar benefits can be derived from playing board games, strategy and business simulation games where long-term planning is key, including RISK, Chess, Monopoly, Theme Park World and Rollercoaster Tycoon. Nowadays, there are even more to choose from, for example, Coffee Tycoon, Game Dev Tycoon and Transport Tycoon, to name a few. Start with one and see if it sparks the imagination.

My father encouraged me to play chess because you learn strategy and must always plan ten steps ahead of the game.

Ana Kovziridze, Skinovation Medspa

Play board games like Monopoly. Monopoly is amazing at teaching children how to budget and manage money while having fun.

Alexandra Axsen, Lake Okanagan Realty Ltd.

When growing up, creativity was strongly encouraged when solving problems. My dad, who ran an electrical engineering company, would constantly encourage us to look at patterns, play games with blocks and tools and emphasized hands-on learning. My siblings and I spent endless hours as kids looking at puzzles, number sequences or solving hands-on challenges, always in a fun, engaging environment.

Casey Hill, Hill Gaming Company

PETER THIEL

Known for: Co-founder of PayPal

What else: Thiel became Facebook's first outside investor when he acquired a 10.2% stake for $500,000 in August 2004.

Before settling in California in 1977, the Thiels had lived in South Africa and South-West Africa (modern-day Namibia) and Peter had changed elementary schools seven times. One of Peter's elementary schools, a strict establishment in Swakopmund, required students to wear uniforms and utilised corporal punishment such as striking students' hands with a ruler for mistakes.

During childhood, Thiel was a chess prodigy. He started playing at the age of six and in 1992, he attained a peak rating of 2,342 from the United States Chess Federation. He was awarded the title of Life Master. Thiel also played Dungeons & Dragons, was an avid reader of science fiction, with Isaac Asimov and Robert A Heinlein among his favourite authors, and a fan of JRR Tolkien's works, stating as an adult that he had read *The Lord of the Rings* over ten times during his childhood.

According to lecture notes from a student on Thiel's start-up class at Stanford University, many of the rules of chess can be applied to business. Lessons include knowing the relative value of your team members as you would your chess pieces; knowing the phases of the game and having a plan; talent matters; there is more to success than luck; and studying the endgame.[55]

EXPERIENCING WORK

JODIE

Someone's thoughts become their words. Their words become their attitudes and beliefs, and these become their actions. These actions shape their future. How someone thinks, therefore, is in some way responsible for everything they achieve. How someone thinks about the concept of work is no different.

Many of the individuals we heard from had an early introduction to the world of work. This didn't necessarily mean they had a job. In some examples, conversations around the dinner table were enough to develop commercial awareness and start thinking about what work involves and why businesses exist. Some parents would point out businesses while on walks and encourage an assessment of their purpose. Children also pick up on their parents' attitudes to their work: if they enjoy it, how much effort they put in and the kind of life it allows them to have.

Think back to when you were small and see if you can remember your first impression of what the word 'work' meant. Think of the jobs your parents had or the businesses they ran. Can you remember what they did or what their day-to-day entailed?

Now think of what you do for work at the moment or how you spend your days. If I asked your children about it, how would they answer? Would they know how you spent your time while at work and understand what you went to work to achieve? You could ask them and see what they say.

Growing up, we become familiar with roles we see all the time: teachers, doctors, shopkeepers, police officers. Most kids could give a plausible explanation of what each of these professions does. YouTubers, gamers and footballers are other roles many kids often see, or perhaps they have watched TV shows including characters like Bob the Builder, Postman Pat or Fireman Sam and are aware of what these roles entail.

Have you ever asked a child what they think an entrepreneur or a business person does? You might be surprised. Perhaps they have watched one on television shows like *Dragons' Den* or *The Apprentice*. Or they could have seen Lord Business in *The Lego Movie*. Hopefully their impression is a positive one, but it could easily not be.

When I was younger, I thought my dad sold cars. Then I found out he managed car dealerships and taught his salespeople to sell cars. Then I found out he was regularly transferred between dealerships to turn around those that were failing and make them profitable again. Then I found out much of his work involved developing his teams and motivating them to do a great job. The older I was, the more detail he went into, which was perfect for developing my understanding of his role. Five-year-old me wouldn't have understood the complexities of people management, but she knew what a car was and understood the concept of making a purchase.

I had a little more experience of my mum's work because she worked from home. I knew she made phone calls and people called to speak to her. I didn't know who she was talking to or what she was talking about, but I knew the calls were important because when my sister and I were too loud we would hear, 'Shhh...' and have to be quiet.

Experience of a working environment can be an interesting experience for kids who otherwise have limited knowledge of what they are. I remember being fascinated by my dad's work. We got to sit in the cars that were for sale, use the photocopier, see the workshop where the cars were fixed and welcome new deliveries from the factory. It meant my understanding wasn't just what my dad and his colleagues did at work, it was an insight into how the entire business worked. Even from being there, playing with the hot chocolate machine and photocopying my face, I was absorbing how the dealership operated, how it made sales and delivered the products. I observed salespeople shaking hands and laughing with customers and the workplace became a new point of reference.

Many schools incorporate work experience at age fifteen or sixteen, but I believe that's too late to begin understanding what work involves. It's also probably the last thing you want to spend your time doing at that age. Bringing your child to work as early as possible can give more context to other concepts included in this book, like supply and demand. Here are some ways to introduce the subject and make it happen.

ACTIONABLES

- Within a school holiday, if it's possible, allocate a day to bring your kids to work with you. Plan in advance what they will do, or who they will meet. Encourage them to think about what they should bring to do while you are working. Perhaps you could set them tasks that will help you.

- If a whole day isn't possible, could you bring them to one meeting or perhaps drop in on a day off to show them around?

- If your company or your business services clients, see if you could take them to see your clients. You'll then be able to talk about the roles of the people you work with and what you do for them.

- Identify friends or family members with interesting roles and see if you can find an opportunity to visit them at work and have them talk to your child about what they do.

- See it through their eyes. Your workplace might be ordinary for you, but it could be an eye-opening experience for them.

- Pay attention to Daddy Pig in the children's cartoon *Peppa Pig*. His job as a structural engineer is quite complicated, but when he takes Peppa and George to his office they always have lots of fun. Season two, episode twenty-two is called 'Daddy Pig's Office'. You could use this to spark a conversation about bringing your kids to work with you.

- Explore museums or heritage sites that are also workplaces. For example, Birmingham's Jewellery Quarter has a pen museum, a jewellery workshop museum and a coffin museum. Each is an example of a workplace in action.

- Talk about these experiences of work in terms of their future and the work they'd like to do. If you're talking about the business premises, for example, a cool office you've seen, talk in terms of the kind of premises they will build for their teams. Assume that they will own the business and discuss accordingly.

My sons spend a lot of time at my office when they're out of school. Instead of hiding them away in a spare office or conference room, I encourage them to greet everyone when they come in, both staff and guests, and they are both learning the power of a confident introduction and 'networking'. I remind them often that hard work is important, but that who you know is also a big influence on your success, so meet people and be helpful, always.

Courtney Barbee, The Bookkeeper

I now lead the global operations of SIS International Research, the company that was founded by my mum, Ruth Stanat, over thirty-five years ago. Since I was six, she took me to business meetings around the world. I travelled with her to Asia and Europe and went to trade shows at a young age. I learned how to conduct myself in meetings, presentations and trade shows. She instilled in me a passion for global business, travel and the consulting lifestyle.

Michael Stanat, SIS International Research

Since I was young, my parents worked from home running the first mail order baseball card business and then record business. My mom said she'd put me in a crib in the living room where my father had his desk and my parents worked. I also was recruited to help sort baseball cards and help out in my dad's store when I was a kid. I always saw my dad working hard at his desk in the living room and often did homework from the living room while he fielded phone calls and shipped records. I helped take packages to the post office when I wasn't in school. I'm sure that seeing my parents working hard and from home in such a visible place helped me become an entrepreneur.

Jennifer Yeko, Ninja Recruiting

MILTON HERSHEY

Known for: Founder of Hershey's, now one of the world's biggest confectionery manufacturers

What else: Milton and his wife Kitty were booked to travel on the Titanic, but fortunately cancelled their trip at the last minute.

By the time Hershey turned thirteen he had attended six different schools. Hershey's father, Henry, was a dreamer who was constantly starting new jobs and working on his next 'get rich quick' scheme. His mother, Fanny, was a devoted Mennonite.

Like many rural young people of the time, Milton was expected to help out on the family farm, and he learned of the value of hard work and perseverance early on. After the fourth grade, Hershey's mother decided he should leave school and learn a trade. She found him a job as an apprentice to a printer. He would help set up each letter for the printing press and then load the paper and ink for the printer. However, Hershey thought this work was boring.

After spending two years with the printer, his mum helped him find a new apprentice job with a confectioner, where he learned the craft of creating confections. Not long after, and still a teenager, Hershey borrowed $100 from his aunt and opened his first candy shop. After a turbulent time running a business in the confectionery industry, Hershey started to specialise in caramel. After successfully building his caramel business, he sold it in 1900 for one million dollars (over $30 million today) and turned his attention to milk chocolate, which at that time was a luxury product. Hershey was determined to develop a formula for milk chocolate and market and sell it to the American public. [56]

WORK PROJECTS

JODIE

John Maynard Keynes was a British economist during the twentieth century and his ideas, known as Keynesian economics, served as the standard economic model throughout the Great Depression as well as World War II and the post-war economic expansion.[57]

Keynes proposed that governments should stimulate demand during economic downturns by, in effect, paying people to dig holes in the ground and then fill them back up. He thought that public investment would restore full employment even in extreme cases when spending had no social value.

On paper it makes sense, but in real life there are side effects. Let's imagine that workers were actually paid to dig holes in the ground and then fill them up. Day after day they carried out arbitrary tasks just to warrant a salary so that they could spend it for the benefit of the economy. This work wasn't creative or exciting or purposeful, it was just gruelling manual labour. How happy would they be? How fulfilled would they be? How long would they keep doing it for?

Before involving your kids in projects at your work, consider the context. Your work will involve a series of regular tasks with different complexity levels that all lead to overarching goals that contribute to the mission of your business. Perhaps it's the same processes each week or perhaps you work to deadlines or on specific projects. These individual projects likely serve a specific purpose or service a particular need for a client or customers.

Understanding your work and projects on a micro-level will help deepen their understanding of why your work or business exists, and why you can earn a living doing what you do. Without understanding the *why* of your work or business, any projects your kids are involved in will feel akin to digging a hole and filling it back up again.

ACTIONABLES

Use this four-step process of discussions as the basis for ascertaining which projects you can get them involved in. Start with those they naturally gravitate towards.

Understanding why you do what you do. Talk to them about:

- Who your work is for
- What your work achieves
- How your work helps people

Understanding what your colleagues do to achieve goals. Talk to them about:

- The individuals involved and their responsibilities
- How they work together to ensure work is completed
- What happens if something isn't completed
- How each person contributes to the company's bigger goals

Understanding how they can help you achieve those goals. This might involve:

- Drawing your role out on a big sheet of paper and writing down everything you do (draw arrows to show which actions lead to other actions and other interdependencies)
- Talking about inputs and outputs and what it means when you do your job well
- Breaking up each area of everything you do into micro-tasks
- Looking out for areas that pique their interest or that they ask more questions about
- Choosing some tasks that they could help you with

When you have identified an area of your work they can help you with, discuss:

- Which skills are required to deliver that task
- What makes a job well done and what makes a job unfinished
- How they could be trusted to do it well

Alternatively, you could adopt the phrase 'let's just try', and test out different tasks with the sole goal of developing a basic understanding and building that into expertise and ownership.

I think the biggest thing to help kids understand entrepreneurship is giving them visibility into as much as possible. Talk to them about everything you go through. The marketing campaigns. The proposals. The client management. Creative work. Hiring the right people. You never know what's going to excite or interest them, so expose them to as much as possible. It could spur an interest or a career pursuit in something specific, or maybe they like the idea of creating and running their own business. And hey, even if they don't and they work for someone, they will grow an appreciation for what entrepreneurs go through, and have a deep respect for their own leaders.

Tessa May Marr, Mad Media

This summer I brought my five-year-old son to work with me. He was excited about going to work like his dad! I started off giving him a daily task list of what he needed to do for pre-determined dollar amounts, just like I would with an employee. Then I asked him how would he solve problems for other people at the company. Little things, like asking employees if they needed the floor cleaned or their trash emptying. Getting your kids thinking about how to solve problems for others is the first step to them thinking like an entrepreneur.

Curt Doherty, CNC Machines

When I was really little, my dad was miserable at his job, despite spending his twenties working his way up to a VP at a local property management firm. He spent every lunch break driving around Portland looking for potential properties to buy and, with a partner, slowly started investing. He was able to quit his job at thirty-five, when I was seven years old, and I got to watch his life change. In this new venture running his own small business as a landlord, he gave me odd jobs that played to my strengths throughout my childhood, like creating and sending holiday cards to his tenants and contractors.

Chelsea Cole, A Duck's Oven

SOCIAL MEDIA MANAGEMENT

JODIE

One of my social media agency's favourite clients is a family soft play centre called Little Green Frog Cafe. Ben, the cafe's owner, is determined that his kids are involved with the family business. He can see all of the future benefits to them of understanding how everything works and having parts of the operations that they can be responsible for.

When my agency worked with Ben and his family on the cafe's opening launch campaign, we thought about how we could involve Ben's four children with the social media updates. They were each familiar with Facebook in a personal sense, having seen their mum's account, but using it to promote their family cafe was another story.

Here are the ideas we came up with together:

- Tasking the kids with taking photos of the cafe. This links to the idea of attracting customers, who will see pictures of the cafe and want to visit. We talked about the kind of photos that might attract new customers to the cafe as well as who would take them.

- Tasking them with sharing 'what's new'. A new menu item, a new area, a new toy. We helped them to understand that new information is interesting to those people who are following a company on social media.

- Tasking each child with finding pictures of frogs. The name and theme of the cafe is frogs, so we discussed how we can talk about frogs and make them interesting. This led to lots of ideas for frog-related things we could post: famous frogs, cute frog pictures, frog facts, frogs in films and so on.

ACTIONABLES

Setting the scene:

🚀 After discussing how businesses work, what a business is there to do, and hopefully giving them some experience of a workplace in action, move the conversations to talking about how businesses attract customers.

🚀 Introduce the concept of marketing by noticing when marketing is happening around you. For example, billboards: What is the message? Who are they trying to sell to? Do you think it's a good billboard? Why or why not?

🚀 Introduce the jargon. Teach them marketing phrases such as 'call to action' or 'value proposition' or 'features and benefits' and turn spotting them into a game.

🚀 Discuss advertisements on the radio and television.

🚀 Read newspapers and magazines and spot the difference between an advert and a feature.

🚀 Look up some brands you regularly interact with on social media. What information do they share? What are they trying to teach you? What is the purpose of the information they are sharing? Do you like it?

🚀 When you're out, look at everyone looking at their phones. What are they doing on their phones? They're most likely on social media. Talk about what this means for those brands that are sending out social media posts.

🚀 Introduce the concept of *consuming* social media updates versus *producing* social media updates. One can grow your business, the other likely just wastes your time.

🚀 Provide context by talking about the above in relation to your own work or to a brand they are familiar with. Ensure they understand why a business might use social media, to lead on to specifics on what they can talk about.

How kids can learn social media management:

- Practise. Set up a private Twitter account with a pretend company name where they can tweet to their heart's content as if they were representing that business. Get creative about the kind of business it could be.

- Talk about planning social media posts. Create a template for a social media content plan that they can fill in with different topics for each day.

- Talk about how a business can be represented in pictures. If there's an interest in photography, develop the interest into commercial photography. Talk about what customers want to see before they make a purchase.

- Earlier we talked about journaling the day's events. Imagine you are a travel, lifestyle or food blogger. How can you turn your journals into articles that other people will be interested to read? Understanding the difference between writing personally and writing commercially is key to social media management.

Today, I am the founder of our family company, that is named for my grandmother, Dorita. I decided it was important to involve my children in the transition from me having a job to starting a business. First, so that they could understand how the transition would affect the lifestyle they were accustomed to with my previous job, and second so that they could help me and my husband succeed. Since, my two oldest boys who are ages thirteen and fifteen have been helping me run my Facebook, Instagram and YouTube accounts and have recently begun learning how to take videos for my social feeds as well. I figure, if they are going to be obsessed with social media, they might as well put their time on it to good use.

Josephine Caminos Oria, La Dorita Cooks Kitchen Incubator

I helped my eldest daughter launch her first business at nine years old, and the benefits have been immeasurable. She's doing better in school, has improved her self-esteem and we have a fun project to bond over. Since that time, I've begun involving all of my kids in entrepreneurial activities. They're all working together to produce their first podcast, my ten-year-old has a website where she reviews children's books, and my seven-year-old just launched a YouTube channel.

Meg Brunson, FamilyPreneur Podcast

My kids are involved in my business because we teach kids to cook. So quite often, they'll be part of Instagram stories and even on live TV, which has pushed them to be comfortable speaking in public. They also get to see the results on social media when people comment, which I feel helps build their confidence. My eleven-year-old daughter helps with social media statistics once a week, and my fourteen-year-old son is our video editor. He's been hard at work recently editing a series of videos for social media and has had to learn the fine art of being concise. The feedback we keep receiving from colleagues is, 'Shorter, shorter, shorter!' The social media internet attention span is not good, and he's having to work with that by brutally cutting every non-essential second.

Katie Kimball, Kitchen Stewardship LLC and the Kids Cook Real Food eCourse

SELLING IN PRACTICE

JODIE

I interviewed Deepak Tailor, founder of website Latest Free Stuff, for the Clever Tykes podcast and asked about his inspiration for setting up his site.[58] The answer? Discovering eBay from a young age and realising that he could sell unwanted items that were around the house to make money. He started small. At first, it was things that were about to be taken to a charity shop or stored in an attic. He would take pictures and write descriptions and then be amazed when he received bids from all over the country. His mum was happy that he was helping to keep the house tidy and she was fascinated that her trash could be someone else's treasure.

Back then, eBay was the site of the moment, but now there are numerous options for selling online, most of which provide a risk-free way of becoming familiar with the actions and terminology associated with it.

Other ways to explore selling online:

- Look up books you want to clear out on Amazon and click, 'Have one to sell? Sell on Amazon' to list yours. This also works for electronics and other household items.

- Look out for neighbours having clear-outs or garage sales and ask if you can partner with them to list their items online. Agree a percentage split and compile a spreadsheet with the items and their sale prices.

- Older children might have creative pursuits that include fashion, writing or art, which can be listed on Etsy, eBay, Amazon, Depop and others. Look around those sites together and ask, 'What would your store look like?' or 'What could you create to sell here?'

- 🚀 Even just browsing sites such as Etsy can open up someone's imagination when considering what they can create to sell. Sellers on Etsy are designing wall prints, cushions, plant pots, upcycled furniture and thousands of other items that people are looking to buy.

Selling in practice doesn't have to be online. Another option is an organised car boot sale or flea market. The benefit of in-person sales is the real-life and real-time experience of supply and demand, understanding the needs of others and negotiation. Selling at these events can be a great chance to practise people skills and develop confidence.

Steps to practise in-person selling:

- 🚀 Research car boot sales or flea markets happening nearby and put them in the calendar.

- 🚀 Identify unwanted items and store them together in a box or specific place so it's clear what can be taken to an event to sell.

- 🚀 Prepare. Make a list of everything you will need: A table, a clothes rail, price tags, shopping bags and a kitty. What else?

- 🚀 Think about how you will present your items for sale so they are more likely to look appealing to buyers.

- 🚀 Practise. Before the event, talk about what will happen when you're there and role-play conversations, including haggling.

- 🚀 Bring a notepad to record everything you have spent or made. Include any entry fee, money spent on lunch as well as what you made from sales of items.

- 🚀 If these steps seem too daunting, attend as an observer first. Notice how stands are laid out and how items are displayed. Notice what people say and how sellers attract customers and make sales.

ACTIONABLES

How to ignite an interest in eBay selling:

- ✦ Identify unwanted items and store them in a box or specific place, so it's clear what can be included in any sales.

- ✦ Explore the site together. Look at other people's listings of items that you own and see how much they sold for (tick the 'completed listings' box).

- ✦ Do it together. Set aside some time and make a goal of listing five items.

- ✦ Talk through what happens next. If your item sells, how will you get it to the buyer? If your item doesn't sell, what will you do with it?

- ✦ Decide what you'll do with the winnings. Perhaps you could plan a day trip or meal out together. (In Deepak's case, he used the proceeds to buy more items to sell.)

Both my kids show a lot of interest in being entrepreneurs, my daughter mostly as she loves to sew so I made sure she took fashion in high school and I also bought her a sewing machine. I try to encourage everything that she works on by promoting options of things she can do with her creations, including selling them. She is about to launch her own Etsy account. I do always attempt to make sure that she is aware of the hard work that is required and the possible downfalls along with the positives.

Alina Freyre, Table of Sweets

My husband and I both run small businesses and my son has definitely been bitten by the bug in a natural way. He's exposed to what we do and soaks up more than we realize. We taught him how to list his old toys on Let Go. He takes the photos, decides the price and I ask him to dictate the description. We also discuss pricing and practise giving change.

Stacie Krajchir-Tom, The Bungalow PR

I run a Business Club at school to teach children specific entrepreneurial skills. The children in the club are split into teams and they work towards a planned selling event such as the Christmas Market. They come up with a team name and a logo. Specific positions of responsibility are decided upon such as finance manager, creative manager, production manager. The teams undertake market research to identify products that would be suitable for their potential customers (children and adults who attend the fair). Then they have to apply for a loan. This is done by filling in a form and asking an adult, who will question them, for the money. The maximum loan value is £100. With the money, each team member is given the responsibility of researching and buying the products for their stall.

They design posters, Tweets and assembly presentations to advertise their stalls. On the day, they run the stall entirely on their own, talking to customers, taking money and giving change. They have to set up and tidy up on their own too, thinking about the presentation of their stall and its appeal to customers. After the event, the teams meet once more. At this meeting they count the proceeds, pay back the debt/loan and make a donation to a charity of their choice, a bit of philanthropy! Any profit after this is shared among the team members so they earn real money as a result of their business. The team with the most profit is presented with the Ashbridge Entrepreneurs Trophy...

Karen Mehta, Ashbridge Independent School

INGVAR FEODOR KAMPRAD

Known for: Founder of IKEA

What else: Once he remarked:
'If you work and do not feel incorrigible enthusiasm, consider that at least a third of your life has gone down the drain.'[59]

When Kamprad was growing up, his grandfather's company was on the verge of bankruptcy, leading him to have difficulty paying the mortgage and finally committing suicide. Kamprad's grandmother, however, managed to save the business. In doing so she taught her grandson to bridge over difficulties with willpower and perseverance. He also says she protected him from the outside world. Before his death, Kamprad and his grandfather were close. Kamprad used to run errands for him, and his grandfather encouraged his imagination and made him believe that anything was possible.

Kamprad began his career at the age of six, selling matches. From the age of ten, he rode around the neighbourhood on his bicycle, selling Christmas decorations, fish and pencils. When Kamprad was seventeen, his father gave him a cash reward for succeeding in his studies.

'In the field of business, I guess I was a little different from the others, as I started to show business activity very early. My aunt helped me to buy the first one hundred boxes of matches on the sale of so-called "88 Øre" in Stockholm. The whole package was worth 88 øre, and my aunt did not even make me pay for postage costs. After that I sold a box of matches at a price of 2 or 3 øre and some at 5 øre. I still remember the pleasant sensation experienced by receiving my first profit. At the time, I was no more than five years old.'[60]

He was neither trained to do business, nor did he read books on the subject. Kamprad, who was also dyslexic, described himself as a drop-out, but always replaced his lack of a university degree with enthusiasm. He also made the best use of his time. According to Kamprad, 'You can do so much in ten minutes' time. Ten minutes, once gone, are gone for good. Divide your life into 10-minute units and sacrifice as few of them as possible in meaningless activity.'[61]

SERVICES

JODIE

Business models that involve buying and selling are easy to conceptualise. Exchanging money for tangible goods and calculating the cost and profit of each sale is a great starting point to establish an understanding of business. Schools that hold bake sales or summer fetes often introduce kids to the buying and selling of inexpensive products. Examples of buying and selling goods arise in basic financial education. Lemonade stand, anyone?

Service-based businesses, however, require a completely different level of understanding. Paying for a service usually involves the exchange of money for time and expertise, or for the completion of a certain task. Working out profit must account for the investment of all inputs.

The first story in the Clever Tykes series is *Walk-it Willow*, a story about a dog walking venture. Providing a service can be an accessible first step for kids to start experiencing work. Depending on their age, they can do chores around the house, babysitting, gardening or offer to wash cars for the neighbours, which are all ways to experience trading time for money. Willow's story also introduced the idea of scale. Willow isn't limited to walking one dog at a time, so she isn't limited in what she can earn. Further down the line, she explores how she can ask a friend to help her and grows her dog-walking business.

When I was younger, I used to babysit for a family down my road and I was paid by the hour. Sometimes the family went on their evenings out with another family, so I had double the children to look after and was paid double. When I worked as a waitress, I was paid by the hour but the better I was at my job the more I earned in tips. Thinking like a business owner involves moving away from hourly rates and towards those that are outcome-based or scaleable, and this can be sparked in discussions about services.

When I interviewed Graham Allcott, bestselling author of *How to Be a Productivity Ninja*,[62] he told me about when he and a friend washed their neighbours' cars in exchange for money. They quickly worked out that what their customers expected was a clean and polished car, including more tricky places like the wheels and roof. Together they developed a system for achieving this outcome in the quickest time possible, then they would go back and collect their money. However, sometimes the customer would think they had washed the car too quickly, and that it couldn't possibly be clean enough. Graham soon learned to wash all the cars first and collect the monies at the end of the day so that the customer disassociated their satisfaction with time outlay.

ACTIONABLES

- Think about your neighbours' needs. What services do they require? What do they need help with? What do they grumble about?

- Look at your resources. How can you put them to use? (A bike, a skateboard, car washing equipment or loads of enthusiasm.)

- What would a successful service look like?

- Discuss scale. If it went really well, how could you grow it?

- Who would you approach first?

- Map out the steps together, including who you will approach, what you will offer and how you will charge for the service you are providing.

- Pre-empt hearing a 'no'. Not everyone will want their car washing, and that's fine. Hearing a 'no' isn't something to be taken personally – it's all part of the game.

My parents would support me in my efforts. So, if I was selling something, they would make a purchase and walk with me as I walked our neighborhood going door-to-door. I'd approach the neighbors' doors on my own, but they would be there waiting for me on the sidewalk. I was encouraged to have the face to face 'meetings' on my own, which developed my social interactions, including establishing good eye contact, making a cohesive pitch, being comfortable talking with strangers, and expressing gratitude (whether the person bought something from me or not). These are all skills that I use today as an entrepreneur.

Romy Taormina, Psi Bands

My parents were very encouraging of my entrepreneurial endeavors. In my very early years I'd sell lemonade, cotton candy and even once tried to sell time-shares to tents in my parents' backyard, which they quickly shut down.

Joshua Evans, Culture Consulting Associates

I am continually asking my children to look for ways to be entrepreneurial by looking for a need in our community they can meet for profit. When they were younger, they decided to make and sell Fourth of July T-shirts at our town's annual parade. They budgeted the cost of plain T-shirts and spray paint and determined a good price point for the final product. They made the shirts together and created a stand to sell them and had a lot of fun making some money together. They've also looked to do other things like create a dog-walking business and selling chocolate chip cookies on the sidewalk.

Donna Bozzo, author of *Fidget Busters*

I grew up in a small town in western New York. One of my dad's co-workers did some farming on the side, and he had a large flower patch that bloomed each year. When I was around ten years old, I was looking to make some extra money to buy new baseball cleats, so my dad suggested I offer to cut his friend's flowers and sell them on the side of our road. I followed his advice and was able to make $63 in a day's work, which felt like a million at the time. That was my first taste of entrepreneurship and really planted the seed to seek other opportunities once I was older.

Michael Wittmeyer, JM Bullion, Inc

JOHN PAUL DEJORIA

Known for: Co-founder of the Paul Mitchell line of hair products and The Patrón Spirits Company

What else: With a net worth of US $2.7 billion (2020),[63] in 1980 he formed John Paul Mitchell Systems with hairdresser Paul Mitchell and a loan for $700 while living in his car.

DeJoria was the son of an Italian immigrant father and a Greek immigrant mother, and grew up in a Los Angeles neighbourhood. His parents divorced when he was two years old. According to DeJoria, he learned about basic survival after his parents were divorced and at age six he joined a gang in East Los Angeles. When his single mother proved unable to support both children, they were sent to a nearby foster home, visiting their mother only at weekends.

'My first job, nine years old, part-time, was selling Christmas cards door-to-door. Ten years old, my brother and I had paper routes. We delivered a morning paper called the *L.A. Examiner.* Get up at 4 o'clock, fold your papers, deliver them and get ready for school.'[64] DeJoria entered the world of hair care as an entry-level employee of Redken Laboratories, a position he was later fired from.

SPORT

JODIE

Today's sports professionals such as Serena Williams, Cristiano Ronaldo and Katie Taylor aren't just playing their sport – they are marketing themselves as brands. Even without the global fame these particular athletes have amassed, there are transferable skills to be gleaned from playing a sport, on and off the pitch, court, track or stage.

Playing any sport as part of a team develops teamwork, communication and decision-making skills. It might help someone deal with pressure, learn how to stay level-headed, compete fairly and to the best of their ability, and learn how to focus on what is in their control. All of these skills and abilities have direct carryover to the world of business.

ACTIONABLES

How to encourage sport in your children's lives:

🏹 **Watch sport together:** Make the most of the Olympics or various sporting world cups being shown on television by watching them together and talking about trying out the sports you see. Make plans to try it out while the enthusiasm is high. The more accessible the sport, the easier it becomes to develop a habit that sticks.

🏹 **Find local sports clubs:** A quick Google search should reveal some nearby clubs and most will offer taster sessions to introduce the basics. Overcome barriers to starting by emphasising that it's a one-off exploratory exercise that doesn't necessarily need to be a regular occurrence. Take baby steps to ensure trying a new sport isn't met with resistance.

- 🚀 **Lower the expectations:** Seeing people who have been playing a certain sport for a while might seem daunting at first, but explain the learning curve involved in anything, and reassure them that there's no reason they couldn't be as good as more advanced players in the future.

- 🚀 **Have another purpose in mind:** Sport doesn't have to be undertaken for sport's sake. Martial arts, for example, is great for learning self-defence. You could set goals or targets together as a family, and encourage each other to achieve them.

- 🚀 **Talk about sportspeople:** Sportspeople can be fantastic role models to ignite interest and keep someone motivated to improve in their chosen sport. When discussing specific footballers or athletes, talk about their daily routine, what they might practise and how often, how they keep improving and how much they enjoy what they do.

- 🚀 **Consider physical education just as important as other subjects:** Remember PE at school? It was rarely seen as a serious subject because it didn't have exams and coursework, but regarding it with the same importance as core subjects will help it not be overlooked.

We re-enforce that in order to do well, you need to practise your sport. We don't want our children to think that just because they participate, that they are going to automatically win. When they lose games, we ask them what they learned from the experience.

Doug Dibert Jr, Magnfi

I played competitive soccer until I was eighteen, mostly with the same group of guys. We achieved a lot of success for young people. Naturally, to achieve this success we had great players, but more than that we had dedicated, hard-working and ambitious players, some of whom play professional soccer in the MLS today. We trained three to four times per week, usually at night, and had extremely high expectations for one another. We learned the importance of time management, account-ability, dedication, teamwork and myriad other values. If it wasn't for my experiences with that soccer club, I would not have built the necessary life skills to become a successful entrepreneur.

Jeff Rizzo, RIZKNOWS LLC

I was always involved in team sports like soccer, cross-country and track and my dad always told me that being a good team member would serve me well in life. It turns out my parents prepared me well for life as an entrepreneur and gave me the confidence, risk tolerance and encouragement I needed to be persistent and resourceful.

Paige Arnof-Fenn, Mavens & Moguls

ARNOLD SCHWARZENEGGER

Known for: Athlete, actor, politician

What else: Seven-time Mr Olympia and four-time Mr Universe.

Growing up in Austria, at school Schwarzenegger was reportedly academically average, but stood out for his lively character. Schwarzenegger grew up with a father whose answer to life was discipline. He and his brother followed a strict routine under their father's watch. Their chores included sports and specific exercises, and family meals such as breakfast were 'earned' by doing sit-ups. Each day, after the chores were complete, it was time for soccer. This would happen no matter what the weather, and their father was known for shouting when mistakes happened during practice. In 1960, Schwarzenegger's soccer coach took the team to a nearby gym, and the weight training fascination began.

In his book, *Total Recall*, Schwarzenegger remembered that their father believed just as strongly in training their brains as their bodies. They would visit different villages and spend their time reading books and seeing plays.

BUSINESS PLANNING

JODIE

Planning a business from scratch is so much fun. Stumbling upon a great idea then working out how it could be turned into a real-life venture is one of my favourite pastimes. Even if I don't start the business, I enjoy the exercise in itself. Coming up with ideas and evaluating their commercial feasibility is what entrepreneurs are doing multiple times per day.

When to write a business plan with your son or daughter:

- When they have come up with a great idea on how to solve a problem.

- When they are looking for ideas on how to make money.

- When they are bored and want something to do.

- When they see a business that already exists that they would like to own.

Doing this exercise together develops a deeper understanding of how a business works and encourages creativity as well as strategic and commercial thinking. It might also help spark excitement about what can be achieved with ambition and planning.

The example plan included here can be made as simple or complex as is suitable. The business could also be tied into something they really enjoy such as their favourite snack, toy or hobby. The idea you plan doesn't have to be brand new – it could be a better version of something that already exists.

You can also download a business planning worksheet at clevertykes.com/book

ACTIONABLES

I recommend that you complete the template together at first and, when they've gained some confidence, let them get started and just help them fill in the gaps. Perhaps print several of them so they're always to hand when an idea is thought of.

Example Business Plan

Name: _____

Date: _____

Business name: _____

What problem does your business solve?
_____

What does your business do?
_____

Who is your target audience?
_____

How will you sell your product or service?
_____

How will people find out about your business? *[Marketing plan including value propositions, key messaging, advertising]*
_____

Funding required to begin, and what it will be used for? *[Fixed and variable costs, time taken to break even]*

_____

Sale price of your product or service? *[How much it costs to produce, profit made per unit]*

_____

As an entrepreneur myself, I have always sought to teach my children how to be entrepreneurial. I work from home so it's easy for them to see my work and what it entails. My eldest son was three when he started to take a great interest in also starting his own company one day. We started simple and I asked him what kind of company he'd like to have. He wanted to make toy trucks. I suggested that they would have to have something special that would set them apart from the competition. Then I told him that he would have to find a designer to work with as well as a factory where the trucks could be made. We also discussed shipping and retailers and the entire process. I broke it down into kid terms and he was fascinated. I have had similar conversations with my six-year-old who has an interest in building. It is an ongoing conversation during school runs as they both are interested in creating things.

Caryn Antonini, Early Lingo, Inc

My daughters wanted to earn some money, so we figured out a way for them to start their own little business when they were seven and eight years old. We brainstormed ways they could earn money, read books on entrepreneurship for kids, and watched all of the videos found on the *Secret Millionaires Club*. My daughters turned their love of crafts into their little business. They sell their crafty creations at a local farmers' market. Not only have they learned about the business aspects, but they have also learned other skills such as sewing, knitting on a loom and creating additional crafts. They know that they make more of a profit if their expenses are lower resulting in some unique Christmas gift suggestions. My husband and I have offered to pay for them to sell at the local farmers' market a set number of times as a Christmas gift, and they have also received supplies for their crafts as gifts from family. They purchase any other additional supplies using their own money. Overall, they have learned a lot from this experience while making some money to donate, spend or save for future expenses.

Brigitte Brulz, author of *Jobs of a Preschooler*

My daughter is really into homemade masks and potions. She does her research in terms of the ingredients and their benefits and then prepares wonderful items. We really encourage her inclination and have taught her about creating a business case and then a company, about sourcing ingredients and also making a social impact.

Preeti Adhikary, Fusemachines Inc

PART 4
THE PARENT-MENTOR

DANIEL

Kids do silly things. They frequently act without care for consequences. They break things, they believe almost anything they are told and they can express ridiculous ideas. They are completely unaware of how little they know about the world and they often ooze confidence despite clearly being out of their depth.

Don't get me wrong – that's a big part of what we love about kids. We love their naivety; we love their pure optimism and their cheekiness. As parents, however, it's our job to help kids successfully navigate the world and pick up valuable lessons along the way.

As a parent, guardian or educator you can correct them constantly by giving them the answers, telling them what to do and highlighting their shortcomings in a direct way. It's easier and faster to simply think for your kids rather than painfully teaching them to think for themselves – at least in the short term.

In the long term though, you don't want to think for your kids. You want them to become self-aware, insightful and refined in their choices. You want your kids to develop critical thinking skills, good habits and an ability to reflect meaningfully on their decisions.

As parents, you face a daily challenge: to either give your child answers and directions or to teach them to come up with the right behaviours and ideas themselves. Mentoring is the latter. It's the hard work of shaping your kids through asking questions rather than giving commands.

As a teenager I took a particular dislike to a certain teacher at school and I disengaged from the subject. My father took me aside one afternoon and said, 'It seems like you are going to fail this class as a way of showing this teacher how much you don't like him. Do you think that strategy is the best way to get your message across?'

We talked about it and I realised that I was about to inflict poor grades on myself to punish a teacher who really didn't care about failing me or not. My father said, 'It's OK if you fail this subject but I think you would find it frustrating having to repeat it, especially if you got the same teacher again, but the choice is yours.' Through some carefully worded questions, I gained perspective on the situation and realised that passing the subject was a better strategy.

All humans have built-in decision-making capabilities. Through my work with thousands of entrepreneurs, I get to see people wrestling with tough choices and I've observed that it's almost as if there are three brains trapped inside each person's head.

The first brain is what I call 'the reptile'. It's the angry, tantrum-throwing, sobbing, nasty, aggressive, fearful part of ourselves. Traditionally we've known this part of the brain as the 'fight, flight, freeze' response but more recently we've come to know it as that part of ourselves that gets 'triggered'. This reptile brain causes drama and strife and derails what would have been a successful plan.

The next part of the brain I see regularly is 'the autopilot'. It's the part of the brain that mindlessly scrolls through social media or the part that can drive a car while you are thinking about other things. It's the part that makes breakfast for you in the morning, ties your shoes or responds to simple emails. This is the part of you that loves the status quo – it would be perfectly happy if your life revolved around menial tasks and mindless entertainment.

The third part of the brain is 'the entrepreneur' or 'the visionary'. This part of the brain contains endless storms of creativity, strategy, love, empathy, compassion, cleverness and inspiration. Everything wonderful in your life – your best ideas, your deepest conversations, your smartest solutions to difficult problems come from this place.

I don't think I am overstating it when I say that the success of your children's futures comes down to them, on balance, making the most of their visionary mindset and being able to artfully manage the reptile moments when they arise.

Being a great mentor to a kid is often about tipping things back in the favour of the visionary mindset. Children under seven years old are especially geared to 'go reptile' and throw a tantrum for almost any reason. A parent might view a tantrum as naughtiness and try to discipline the child whereas a mentor might see a tantrum as an opportunity to learn how to deal with reptile moments more effectively – such as taking a deep breath or a moment to pause.

As kids get older, it is inevitable that you will get into debates with them. If you can keep your cool and see the bigger picture, these debates are fertile ground for teaching lessons. Like a grandmaster in chess, hold your position firmly in your mind, while also mentoring your kids on how they could improve their position and effectively get their needs met.

Rather than scolding a child for being persistent, let them know that you admire their persistence regardless of whether you change your mind. Rather than saying, 'I gave you your answer and I'm sticking with it,' you could say, 'You've not improved your argument since last time we discussed this, so my answer is the same as before, but here's how you might present your point differently...' This subtle shift lets them know that whingeing and complaining doesn't change things but improving the argument might. In this way, you are being both a parent and a mentor.

At age nine, Jodie arrived at the breakfast table to a special announcement from her mother. 'I've just heard on the radio that today is statistically the happiest day of the year. It's the day most people feel really good and treat each other wonderfully. Today we will measure and see how many happy things happen to us.' Jodie's mum kept this up all day and by bedtime, Jodie agreed that it had indeed been a pretty wonderful day.

It was only then that her mother revealed the truth. The radio had predicted the day as one that was going to be pretty miserable because of the weather and it being the time of the year when most people were returning to work after Christmas. Jodie's mum explained that whether you say it's going to be a great day or it's going to be a miserable day, you'll probably be right. The lesson stuck and to this day Jodie makes a conscious choice that every day is going to be wonderful.

Mentoring your kids can also be about letting them learn from a wide variety of teachers and mentors other than their parents and school teachers. Stepping back while your children ask questions of a family friend who owns a business will allow them to internalise the lessons. Encouraging your children to write an email to someone they consider a hero will send a message that success has fewer barriers than they first thought.

A mentor is someone with real-world experience who actively shapes and guides the beliefs and actions of someone who's still learning the ropes. By definition, a parent or guardian has more real-life experience than their kids and this makes them the most natural person to be their mentor, but the world is full of interesting people who can offer wisdom and guidance to the next generation in a safe setting.

A mentor can sometimes see the bigger lesson or opportunity to grow in a situation. A parent or educator who sees themselves as a mentor might turn a stressful situation into a learning opportunity.

Kids might do silly things but it's so incredible to see how fast they learn and grow with the right mentoring. As any experienced mentor will tell you, it's not a one-sided relationship. As soon as you see yourself as a mentor to a young person, it brings out your best and teaches you valuable lessons about yourself too.

At about thirteen years old, I threw one hell of a tantrum over a bike that I wanted. I had seen the most glorious stunt BMX bike in the shop and was told that there was only one left in stock. I wanted my parents to buy it for me so I didn't miss out. I begged them not to let this perfect bike fall into the hands of another child.

A deal was struck. My parents would buy the bike for me, but it would remain locked up in our garage until I had paid for it in full. Under the terms of the deal, I wasn't even allowed to touch the bike; it was torturous knowing that the forbidden object was under our roof – I had to find a way to pay down the money as fast as possible. This drove me to clean the neighbours' cars and gutters, mow lawns and weed driveways. It took me a month to raise the money and the sense of satisfaction and ownership I felt was immense.

My parents did the right thing. They channelled my desire into something proactive. They took my 'reptile moment' and guided me towards getting resourceful, finding a solution and working hard to make it happen. In that situation, the easy option would be to say no or to buy the bike for me and let me have it. Instead, they were mentors who guided me onto a path full of valuable lessons.

In this section, you will see why the word 'parent' and the word 'mentor' are both nouns and verbs. You are automatically granted the title of 'parent' when you have kids, but you are able to choose the manner in which you parent. Being aware of this and actively playing the role to your best ability will provide your kids with a good model. You are being a mentor if someone is looking up to you for life experience and wisdom and you are engaged in delivering that experience and wisdom thoughtfully.

***

I tell my daughter it's ok to have fear when trying something new, everyone does. What is important is that you try, because how else will you learn? I have fear on a daily basis – of what people think of me, and of what I do, and what I say. However, I push past the fear, and it turns into excitement for 'putting it out there' because mistakes can be 'beautiful'. I explain to her why it's important to believe in herself, not just for her well-being, but for others as well. And to always ask for support when you need it.

Coreyne Woodman-Holoubek, Contracted Leadership

My parents never discouraged me when I failed, they always found ways to bring out the positive in every failure. This encouraged me to analyse why I failed and how I can improve on my failures. In essence, the entrepreneurial spirit is the bold and brave, willing to take chances to achieve what seems impossible. Only those who have the courage to try will ever have the chance at success. My parents taught to not be afraid of failure, but embrace it as a part of life.

Lisa Chu, Black n Bianco

My father taught me not to fear failure. When I was about thirteen years old, he challenged me to disassemble my uncle's VW engine. I didn't know anything about engines and was terrified of doing something wrong. A few days went by and he noticed I hadn't touched it because I was scared of failing or breaking something, so he took me to a junkyard, got another VW engine and took it home. He then said to me, 'I want you to take every single screw, nut and bolt apart from this engine and throw it in a box, and once you throw it in, we'll take it back to the junkyard.' I remember that moment to this day. He created a safe space for me to fail, and taught me to ask myself, 'What's the worst that can happen?' It also taught me to do things differently and to try new things, as long as I was smart about it. He created parameters for experimentation. To add to that, my mother taught me the importance of cultivating relationships and to surround myself with good and interesting people who have camaraderie and are inspirational. I've used both lessons throughout my career, and even in parenthood, and I'm forever thankful for them.

Erich Joiner, Tool of North America

ATTENTION SPAN

JODIE

Mastery is an important element of work satisfaction. Someone being able to master their craft and apply it without interruption will experience a heightened sense of happiness, satisfaction and purpose. Mastery leads to flow, depth and finding the work that feels almost effortless. When I'm working on a book or an article or something I'm enjoying, I love accessing that state of flow that means I am so focused that nothing can disturb me – I feel like I could do it forever.

The opposite of this scenario involves distraction, short attention spans, rushing and multi-tasking, none of which are conducive to progress or fulfilment. Yet the modern world sometimes feels like it better facilitates the latter. Social media, notifications, 'breaking news', interruptions and distractions cost us deep work, mastery and the benefits that they bring. Imagine a dog on a lead, being taken for a walk by its owner. The dog wants to sniff everything and explore for hours, but every time it stops its owner pulls on the lead so it has to follow. 'Come on, we have to go.' If this is replicated with our kids, what will the long-term effect be?

If we can't develop the ability to sit still and focus on something, we are unlikely to develop mastery in any field. Many entrepreneurs are entrepreneurs because they have, at one point, become exceptional at something. Most of the habits and patterns we follow in adulthood have been hard-wired in us by our actions when we were growing up. Focus, concentration and attentiveness are skills to be learned from a young age.

ACTIONABLES

In practice, this might look like:

- Not moving on to a new task until one has been completed.
- Emphasising the importance of completing something.
- Making a big deal of a project being finished (rather than it being perfect).
- Facilitating practice and experimentation rather than setting a goal.
- Allocating more time to activities to allow for flow.
- Planning less in a day to spend more time on each activity rather than fitting to a rigid schedule.
- Intentionally ramping up the time spent on activities to exercise the concentration muscles.
- Modelling how something is done first to enable behaviour mirroring.
- Ensuring the complexity level is sufficiently challenging without being disheartening.
- Being aware of distractions and thinking about how to ignore them.

Whatever [my son is] doing right now, that's the most important thing, so I encourage him to keep doing it as long as possible. I never say, 'Come on! Let's go!' We'll go to the beach or forest, and make things with sticks and sand for half a day before he's ready to switch. Other families come to the playground for twenty or thirty minutes, but we stay there for hours. Nobody else can play with us like this. Everyone else gets so bored.

Derek Sivers, sive.rs

With my own son, at a high level, I think the main thing we've done is to really just follow his instincts and interests and just use those as a platform for encouraging an entrepreneurial mindset. It's really a classical education move; if your kid says they are really into sea turtles you know you just kind of double down on sea turtle stuff! My wife and I both work for ourselves so I imagine there's a certain amount of ambient 'entrepreneur talk' around the home that probably helps, but I feel like the real secret has been just paying close attention to his questions and interests and using those to inspire him.

Mathew Burnett, Super Genius Inc

My parents told me that education was my key to the world, and I could be anything I wanted. The key was to find a passion and love, and consider how my days could be spent doing what I love. They allowed me to travel, even on my own at the early age of eighteen, took me to museums, helped me uncover answers to all of the questions I had as a curious child. They taught me to never stop asking questions, and challenge my mind as often as possible. My parents never forced anything on me, but shared opportunities to learn as often as possible. My father, a businessman, and mother, a teacher, were also passionate about learning themselves, and still spend their days learning about art, literature, music and history. That love for learning, and curiosity, has transcended into my passion for making a difference through the scaling of my business.

Joanne Sonenshine, Connective Impact

JACK DORSEY

Known for: Co-founder of Twitter and founder of Square

What else: In March 2016, Dorsey fully funded about 600 Missouri public school projects registered at DonorsChoose. He walks five miles to work each morning and calls it a 'very clearing time'.

As a teenager, Dorsey loved computers and spent countless hours studying one of the first versions of IBM. He was fascinated with the concept of coordinating taxicabs, couriers, emergency services and other fleets of vehicles and wanted to create a live map of his city, displaying the vehicles in motion as small moving red dots. His passion for cities and towns can be explained by the constant travel of his father, Tim Dorsey, who was an engineer of medical equipment and received many offers across America.

The Dorsey family moved houses multiple times while Jack was growing up. Wherever they had moved in, Jack immediately bought a local map and went on a walk around the city. As a child, he couldn't pronounce any of his words, an impediment that made him feel shy throughout junior high.

According to Dorsey, he could have become an expert in urban planning but his childhood passion for city maps took over. At first, he tried to transfer road atlases into digital format and then, using an electronic bulletin board, put moving objects on his map. The result was a kind of a real city but in miniature. 'I thought the job of a courier must be a kind of magic,' explained Jack. 'I liked to keep track of the physical path of a courier from one point to another or even around the world. Someone takes a package, puts it in a bag, walks somewhere and then hands it to someone else.'[65]

Dorsey's first programming experience occurred when he was fourteen years old when he wrote a few programs for taxi dispatching and firefighting services. He was fascinated with the voices on the police scanner. 'They're always talking about where they're going, what they're doing and where they currently are and that is where the idea for Twitter came,' Dorsey told CBS.[66]

LABELLING

JODIE

Recently I saw a girl aged about nine wearing a T-shirt that read 'I'm not bossy, I have leadership skills'. I loved it. What a perfect example of a positive label compared to one with negative connotations.

The labels applied to us as children stick with us our whole lives. We believe them to be true and we incorporate them as part of our identity, even subconsciously. A child described as clumsy remembers the title when slipping up, starts to believe it's true and creates a self-fulfilling prophecy. In the same way, a child described as useless might give up easier when faced with the next obstacle. With siblings, describing one as 'the academic one' and one as 'the creative one' might seem harmless, but we're not all one-dimensional characters defined by one trait. Someone who is academic can also be creative, and vice-versa, but using labels to differentiate might not be helpful. Besides, does anyone really like being put into a metaphorical box?

As adults, we can choose which labels we use to describe ourselves. We don't take labels that others administer to heart quite as easily because we are certain of ourselves. There's a Robbie Williams song called 'Love My Life' that my mum loves. The lyrics talk about being powerful, beautiful, free, wonderful and magical. If you believe you are all of these things you will walk around feeling that way and you will become that person. If you label yourself as clumsy, ditzy, awkward or silly, you will become that person instead. This isn't about believing you are better than anyone else – because part of recognising and applying labels positively is being able to do it to others too – it's about consistently being the best version of yourself and being able to bring that out in those around you. A line that I love by Jim Cathcart is, 'How would the person I would like to be, do the things I'm about to do?'[67]

My friend Sian has a two-year-old daughter named Imogen. She noticed that whenever others were describing Imogen, no matter what she was doing at the time, it was always about how she looked. 'She's so pretty,' 'isn't she cute?' and 'what a beautiful princess,' were a few of the regulars. Sian realised that these labels would soon become Imogen's inner voice, and she might start to think that how someone looked was their most important characteristic. Sian now makes an effort to only describe her daughter in ways that will empower her actions. She'll use words like 'strong' and other positive adjectives that describe Imogen's character. She also praises her behaviour, focusing on effort rather than outcome, by describing her actions as 'hard-working' or 'patient'.

ACTIONABLES

- Notice when you are administering labels and what the future effect of them will be.
- Differentiate between labelling someone's actions and character.
- Ask your kids what they want to be good at or known for and what's important to them.
- Think of how a negative label could be flipped around to be positive or aspirational.
- Reaffirm the positives by choosing phrases such as 'be confident' instead of 'don't be shy' or 'speak clearly' instead of 'don't mumble'. That way, someone knows how to improve rather than feeling defensive.

Growing up my mother would call me 'the boss'. She would tell me how smart I was.

Alicia White, Project Petals

My dad always encouraged my creative (albeit short-lived) pursuits and used words like 'persistent', 'strong leader', and 'smart' to talk about me, and these were the words I internalized. To this day, he (and my mom, for that matter!) are my 'go-tos' when I'm tossing around a new idea in my head and working hard to give it legs.

Chelsea Cole, A Duck's Oven

Every morning when I left the house for school, my mother would encourage me to 'be brilliant!' That she said this, rather than 'have a nice day!' encouraged me to shine and made it clear that it was up to me to 'show up' every day.

Caren Kelleher, Gold Rush Vinyl

THOMAS EDISON

Known for: An inventor and entrepreneur, Edison founded fourteen companies, including General Electric, still one of the largest publicly traded companies in the world

What else: Edison has many famous quotes related to business, including:

- 'I have not failed. I've just found 10,000 ways that won't work.'
- 'There's a way to do it better – find it.'
- 'Our greatest weakness lies in giving up. The most certain way to succeed is always to try just one more time.'[68]

Edison was born the youngest of seven children. His persistent questioning and hyperactive behaviour did not work well with the other children at school. Thomas stayed in school for about twelve weeks until his short-tempered teacher lost patience with him.

Edison's mother, as he recalled, 'was the making of me... she was always so true and so sure of me... and always made me feel I had someone to live for and must not disappoint.'[69]

Convinced that her son's robust character and unusual physical appearance were purely signs of his remarkable intelligence, Nancy Edison, an accomplished schoolteacher, decided to teach her son at home. Edison obtained most of his early education from RG Parker's scientific textbook *School of Natural Philosophy* and once enrolled for a chemistry course at The Cooper Union for the Advancement of Science and Art.

At the age of twelve, after convincing his parents that he was ready to work, Edison began making money by selling sweets and newspapers on trains. He eventually added vegetables to the list. He turned a $50 a week profit by age thirteen, most of which went to buying equipment for electrical and chemical experiments.

POSITIVITY ABOUT WORK AND MONEY

JODIE

When Daniel's son asked the question, 'How do you make money?' Daniel's response helped set the tone for financial abundance and being creative. He said, 'Well, there are lots of ways to make money. There are all sorts of money opportunities everywhere. There's lots of money out there. There's never been more money around. Sometimes there's money just lying around the house. You might find some down the back of the couch if you get lucky!

'You could do a job for mummy but you could also create something. So, if I wanted to give you some money for a book or a picture that you created then I might buy it off you. If you want to create a beautiful picture for me then I could buy it for a pound and then you could give it to me and then it's mine and I give you the money. And he's like, "Really, I can just create something?" and I'm like, "Yeah, you can!"'

'I'm trying to give him lots of ideas and options as to how this thing called money gets made. And it's not always chores, or doing the bins, cleaning the gutters, and these horrible things... there are all these other ways to create money as well.'

MONEY IS AMAZING!
TAKE MANAGEMENT
ACCOUNTS ... INCREDIBLE!

DANIEL

When kids ask what I do for work, I'm careful about how I respond. The answer I give will shape their mindset about what they will spend a lot of their time doing as adults. If I say that I 'have to' go to work, it makes them think that I am doing so against my will. If I say that work 'pays the bills', I'm creating an impression that work doesn't provide abundance. Telling children that what you do for work is boring, dull, repetitive, frustrating or unrewarding sets them up to believe that's the only way it can be.

What if you flip the script about what work is and tell them that it is a place to succeed, to learn and grow, to meet interesting people and create things? What if you tell your kids that you are excited to start the week and see what interesting problems need to be solved at work? This attitude will rub off and it will open your child's mind to a world of work that is full of passion.

ACTIONABLES

Describe work positively, wherever you can. Work can be:

- Where you go and make things.
- Where you create opportunities.
- Where you talk to people and you come up with ideas on how you can change the world.
- Something you 'get' to do rather than 'have' to do.

I learned at a young age that entrepreneurship and global consulting was a fun way to apply my creative thinking to help brands 'go global', launch new products, create ad campaigns and innovate in meaningful ways that impact the way consumers live. I love writing, and consulting allows me to write, innovate and communicate daily. I learned from my mother that entrepreneurship allows you to 'create' things. She taught me that entrepreneurship meant freedom, freedom to pursue my passions and freedom in choosing projects that were meaningful to me. For much of my life, 'work' actually feels like 'play' as I am passionate about what I do. This has contributed to my success.

Michael Stanat, SIS International Research

When Isabelle was ten years old, she asked me why I kept starting businesses that failed. I was a successful photographer at the time but she was focusing on other things I tried. I was glad that she asked me so that I had the opportunity to explain to her that everything is a learning experience and it's not at all unusual for an entrepreneur to try a lot of businesses before one does really well. Her perspective has shifted very much now that we have a multi-million-dollar business with over 11,000 salespeople. She realizes how important it is to keep going and not give up.

Laura Hunter, LashLiner LLC

I never thought of my dad as an entrepreneur but always as a small business owner. Looking back, even though his father started the car dealership, anyone who runs their own business is an entrepreneur because you're always having to reinvent things. My dad constantly talked about his customers, how he was selling to them, whether he was meeting quotas (and winning trips), and sometimes the difficulty of managing people. He also was incredibly generous, donating an oil change to any event in town and letting sports teams use vehicles to travel for special events, and I remember many weekends and evenings when the phone would ring, and off Dad would go to save someone who had locked their keys in their vehicle. I learned that work is a part of your life, a way you can serve your community, and something to be passionate about and work very hard at. I also learned that complaining about the same managerial problems over and over isn't a good strategy, and every time I catch myself sounding like my dad-the-manager, I know I need to make a change. But if I ever sound like my dad-the-salesman and small business owner, proud of what he did, I smile and know that I'm doing something right.

Katie Kimball, Kitchen Stewardship LLC and the Kids Cook Real Food eCourse

Most of my uncles and cousins worked in construction. I remember helping my Uncle Connie paint houses and being a labourer on my parent's projects. I worked on job sites from the age of twelve and loved working alongside friends and family to build something real; I got satisfaction out of a hard day's work. It was really rewarding building something with your hands and understanding what a hard day's work felt like.

David Broomhead, Trade Hounds

JO MALONE CBE

Known for: Founder of Jo Malone London

What else: In 2006 cosmetic giant Estée Lauder purchased the Jo Malone business for 'undisclosed millions'. She was awarded her CBE in 2018 for services to the British economy, having previously been awarded an MBE.

Malone grew up in a council house in Kent, United Kingdom. She had severe dyslexia and was told at school that she was stupid and lazy, although she knew she was neither. From a 2016 interview with *Woman and Home*:

'We didn't live in poverty but there was certainly not a lot of money around. I never felt I wasn't loved but, my goodness, I was definitely the breadwinner from a very young age... It was my job to make sure that we had food in the cupboard. We had an electric meter and a gas meter and I'd hoard 10p coins up in my room because I knew Dad would take them otherwise, and we needed light and heat when we got home from school. I always had to be two steps ahead in my head.'[70]

Malone's early childhood gave her an early introduction to entrepreneurship. Her mother was a facialist and worked for a woman who owned a small skin-care line marketed under the aristocratic title, Countess Labatti. Malone often went along to the countess's apartment, which served as the company headquarters, and as she recalled, 'When I was nine years old, the countess said to me, "I want you to make your first face mask." And I did, under her tutelage. She also told me, "Life has something very special in store for you, so if you are going to do something, do it brilliantly."'[71]

She also learned entrepreneurial skills from her father, an artist: she accompanied him when he sold his paintings at the local weekend market fair. In her teens, she began making and selling her own T-shirts.

MAKING MISTAKES

JODIE

In the book *The Courage to Be Happy*, Ichiro Kishimi asserts that the goal of education is self-reliance. The art of educating and parenting is to assist at the right time in the right way. Not too soon and not too much but not so late and little as to let someone become disheartened. It can be a tricky balance to strike. In the book, Kishimi discourages praising and rebuking in favour of encouragement, offering assistance and offering words of gratitude. In practice this means:

- ✦ 'I believe you can work this out,' instead of, 'Here's what you should do.'

- ✦ 'If you need my help, ask for it,' instead of jumping in before it's needed.

- ✦ 'Thank-you for helping me with this, it really made a difference,' instead of, 'You did a great job.'

A major component of success is learning from failure. Making mistakes and experiencing failure must be seen in a positive light because it probably means someone's trying something new or really pushing their ability. As adults we know that you've only truly failed once you've given up. Mistakes are just part of a learning curve.

Wherever possible, train the pattern of try, fail, learn, repeat, until you succeed. Then try something new. Live by the rule that you'd rather say, 'I can't believe I did that,' than, 'I wish I did that.' Friedrich Nietzsche said, 'That which does not kill us, makes us stronger.'[72]

In line with Kishimi's teaching, cultivating self-reliance isn't just giving the frameworks and offering the encouragement that means someone can make the right decisions, it's also giving them the chance to learn from the wrong decisions.

ACTIONABLES

Use every mistake or failure as an opportunity to learn by asking these questions:

- 🚀 What happened?
- 🚀 Why did that happen?
- 🚀 What can you do differently next time?
- 🚀 How can you use this as an opportunity?
- 🚀 How can you stop that happening again?
- 🚀 How can you prepare differently?
- 🚀 How would you teach someone else not to make the same mistake?

I tell my daughter often that she's smart and able to do anything she wants if she focuses and sets her mind to it. I also let her try most things herself (as long as it's not dangerous). At only two years old, it's quite funny to see her attempt to carry the shopping bags alone, or zip her coat. When I try to help, she says, 'Mummy I can do it myself,' and she grunts and growls with determination. Then when she's successful she shrieks with happiness, 'Yay, I did it! I did it by myself!'

Ayesha Ofori, PropElle Network

One thing parents can do to instil entrepreneurship in their children is to encourage them to take risks and to actually fail from time to time. For example, if a child has an idea about something that the parent knows won't work, let them do it anyway. Allow them to see it through until they realise it wasn't a good idea, and then be there to support them and encourage other ways to go about doing things.

Andrew Schrage, Money Crashers

I've also learned some important life lessons as an entrepreneur that I am really striving to teach them young – like the lesson that failure is just a learning experience. So, when they 'fail' at something we talk about how that idea didn't work, but it's actually a really great thing that we know that now, and we can think about another idea to try that might work better.

Meg Brunson, FamilyPreneur Podcast

LISTENING TO THEIR IDEAS

JODIE

In improvisational comedy, teams must work together, with no script, to create scenes that will be amusing to an audience. When improv teams practise, there are some rules they follow. The rules are there to ensure the team members work well together and for the act to stand the best chance of entertaining on stage. One of the rules is, 'Yes, and...' This means that if a member of the team starts down a certain path or continues a scene in a certain way, the rest go with it. It requires each other team member to let go of any preconceived ideas they have of how the scene could work.

In *The Office* (US version), there's an episode where the abrasive leader, Michael, goes to an improv class. In one scene that Michael is in, his strategy is to take out a pretend gun and shoot everyone dead. His classmates go along with it, following the 'Yes, and...' rule. Michael's goal is to ensure no one else can speak so that he can perform a monologue and be the star of the show. Here, Michael is taking advantage of everyone else's adherence to the rules of improv, but not necessarily for the benefit of the audience. Have you ever been shut down, interrupted or talked at? It's not fun and not conducive to learning, either.

ACTIONABLES

Taking this framework from improvisational comedy and applying it to home conversations means avoiding one-way monologues. It means that each idea put forward is explored in further detail before being actioned, scheduled or discounted. It means using the words 'Yes. And...' instead of 'No. Because...'

- Yes. And what would happen next?
- Yes. And how would you do that?
- Yes. And when will you do this?
- Yes. And what would that mean?
- Yes. And why do you think it will work?

Instead of:

- No. Because it's a bad idea.
- No. Because you'll spoil your dinner.
- No. Because no one would buy that.
- No. Because your sister thinks it won't work.

The best way of having good ideas is to have lots of ideas and discount all of the bad ones. As grown-ups, we have the benefit of experience. Our years of experience have taught us to instinctively spot a good idea from a bad one, but as a kid, how do you know which are the bad ones? Ideally, you work it out for yourself. You keep going down the path until you realise it won't work.

In applying the principles outlined in this book so far, the goal is to trust that the child with an idea can reach a good conclusion themselves while supporting them to do it, and cultivating a long attention span and independent thinking. They might be going down a rabbit hole but they might be onto something genius, too. Shutting it down means you'll never know, and they are less likely to learn or internalise the conclusion.

Teaching someone the framework for assessing the validity of ideas is something that could put them ahead of most grown-ups, let alone children.

My husband and I try to teach our children the skills that, should they have the desire, will allow them to become entrepreneurs. We do this intentionally and in a number of ways based on our children's current age and maturity level. For example, we allow our five-year-old son to visit our family's decor store and play 'shop'. This helps him build his charisma and people skills through learning how to talk to others in a controlled environment. As we own a storefront, we recently included him in a conversation around how to drive more foot traffic into our store. Our son's idea? Hire a band to play live music so everyone will hear the music and want to come inside! It's not an idea we plan on implementing anytime soon but it was powerful to see how having the opportunity to contribute his ideas gave him a boost of confidence and made him feel like he and his thoughts are valued.

Natasha Smith, Women Run Empires

I always made it a point to be very present in my (fourteen-year-old) son's life even tailoring my career around being available for all of his life milestones. The things we do to foster his entrepreneurial tendencies are number one, we listen to him and his ideas, we say, 'Yes!' more than we say, 'No,' and we empower him to take action and chances.

Kathy Partak, author of *Mason Made: Favorite Recipes*

The question that is critical for all kids to hear to develop the entrepreneur's mindset is, 'What do you think?' All too often we forget to ask kids their thoughts and feelings. We jump into problem solve before they even have a chance to think about the situation.

Julie Smith, adolescent psychotherapist

ENTREPRENEURIAL THINKING ALONGSIDE SCHOOL

JODIE

Some schools are excellent at cultivating enterprising traits in their pupils, providing there are enough teachers championing it and driving it forward. Most schools are not. Understandably, schools focus on exam results and, therefore, are focused on preparing children to score highly in these exams. While they are far from mutually exclusive, most schools do not develop academic prowess in such a way that inspires entrepreneurial thinking. The majority of school exams rely on the recall of information or applications of learned formulae or specific skills, even in the arts subjects.

A good friend is deciding between enrolling her children at the local primary school or overhauling her family life and routine to begin home-schooling. She's not sure that the mainstream school system will be the best route for her kids (or any kids) and she isn't sure that what they will learn will best prepare them for a happy and prosperous future.

I believe that it's possible to equip children with a mindset that will bring an enterprising attitude to the classroom. If someone is taught to think differently, to question and to shape their own path, they can make the most of their school experience and be well-equipped for a successful onward journey.

According to the article 'The Influence of Home on School Success', published by JH Wherry from The Parent Institute, by the time a child is eighteen, less than 14% of their waking hours will have been spent in school.[73] That leaves plenty of time to educate, influence and shape mindsets and actions outside school time. Jim Sheils, author of *The Family Board Meeting: You have 18 summers to create lasting connection with your children*, uses the concept of '18 summers' to explain how you can make use of summer holidays to build deeper connections, reduce device dependency and increase home happiness. [74]

ACTIONABLES

- **Emphasise that there is more to school than lessons:** After a school day, the standard question a parent might ask a child is, 'What did you learn?' Alternatives could be, 'What did you notice today? What surprised you? What did you do better today than yesterday? What did you learn about yourself? Which obstacles did you overcome?'

- **Develop a positive and proactive attitude towards education:** It can be easy to give negative opinions on the topics covered in school, the teaching style of certain teachers, or the homework items brought home. However, consider that openly undermining school might not have the desired effect on how much effort is put in. Being positive and proactive about learning puts it into your and your child's control. Try and respond with answers like, 'Sure, this maths task might be silly, but why don't we be really good at it anyway? You might never revisit this historical event, so learn it once now, really well.' Helping your child identify as someone who is just 'good at stuff' means this can be applied to even the most irrelevant of homework assignments.

- **Make the most of interactions with other kids and teachers:** While lessons might be for listening, learning and writing, there's break time, lunch time and before and after school for developing relationships, emotional intelligence and social skills, including confidence. When discussing school, put equal weighting on these aspects, which include making friends, having a good time and forming character. Teachers can be included in this, as conversing with them is good practice for talking to adults. Ask, 'Who did you spend time with today? Which teachers did you talk to today? What did you learn about others? How did you show kindness?'

As a teacher, and now headteacher, I have always believed in giving children responsibility, asking them to come up with ideas themselves and then letting them get on with it with minimal interference, developing wider, real-life skills outside of the traditional subjects and classroom-based lessons.

Karen Mehta, Ashbridge Independent School

The key is to learn and develop in subjects that interest them. So, don't be a lawyer if you don't want to study law, but if mind reading takes your fancy, then why not do a degree in psychology or forensic science, as my youngest is interested in studying at university. Getting the experience and knowledge in whatever it is they want to do is so important.

Kris Krokosz, Squaredot Ltd

Realising the importance of education, my mother sent me to a very good school – looking back this had both positives and negatives on my 'entrepreneurialism'. On one hand, I learned how to work hard, continually strive for success and to keep pushing to get to the top... and beyond, regardless of what obstacles I was faced with. But I feel I was also moulded to fit society's expectation of what a 'successful' person is... someone who fits the stereotypical business world, which inevitably led me into corporate life once I'd graduated from university. It wasn't until several years later, when I completed an MBA at London Business School, that my entrepreneurial streak was able to be unleashed. It was during those two years where I realised my true calling and I knew that I wasn't made to work for someone else and that, at some point, I would spread my wings and fly solo.

Siddhi Mehta, Rhythm108

READING

JODIE

According to Charlie 'Tremendous' Jones, 'You will be the same person in five years as you are today except for the people you meet and the books you read.'[75]

Think back to some of your favourite books when you were growing up. Chances are, they helped to shape your view of the world and your place within it. I remember intently reading the Famous Five books by Enid Blyton and being inspired to go on adventures and solve mysteries. There weren't many mysteries to solve, so I'd make them up. Many children's and teenagers' books have alternative worlds or realities. They encourage us to use our imagination to picture ourselves there, and to ask, 'What if?'

Entrepreneurs are often visionaries. Their work involves picturing a world, a market or even just their own lives in a completely new way – perhaps one that no one else has ever thought of. No matter what someone's future journey, the written word is powerful. Many roles or gigs are based on writing: content creators, editors, teachers or anyone whose role involves emailing or communicating with others.

Beyond developing imagination and creativity, reading is one of the most effective ways to learn words, develop language skills and absorb information. In books, you can meet and learn from different characters and follow their journeys. I believe there is a time and a place for every type of book – bedtime stories, solo reading or reading in a group. Sometimes it only takes one book to start a passion for reading or for a specific subject.

Here are some recommended reads:

- *Guess How Much I Love You* by Sam McBratney (0–3 years).[76] An early introduction to kindness and looking after each other.

- *The Wonderful Things You'll Be* by Emily Winfield Martin (3–7 years).[77] Sparks thinking about what the future could hold.

- *Oh, the Places You'll Go!* by Dr Seuss (4–8 years).[78] Encouraging readers to find the success they are capable of.

- The Clever Tykes series (6–9 years).[79] These are the books I co-created specifically to introduce children to the positive, entrepreneurial role models that I couldn't find elsewhere.

- *You Are Awesome*, and the *You Are Awesome Journal* by Matthew Syed (9–13 years).[80] Inspires bravery, practice and self-belief.

For teenagers or older children, these are the books I wish I had read while at high school:

- *Awaken the Giant Within* by Anthony Robbins.[81] Teaches powerful frameworks by which someone can set their mind and attitude for success, master their emotions, improve their personal and professional relationships and intentionally set goals.

- *4-Hour Work Week* by Tim Ferriss.[82] I read this in 2012 and it changed my life, including how I viewed wealth, what I wanted to be and how I wanted to spend my time. It introduces the concept of lifestyle design as the foundation from which to build a career or start a business. It helps someone appreciate the value of time and think twice before wasting it.

- *The E-Myth Revisited* by Michael Gerber.[83] A solid introduction to creating and running a business, as well as a digestible explanation of the difference between a sole trader and a company that can scale. The book effectively introduces systems and processes and can provide the inspiration that starts an empire.

- *Atomic Habits* by James Clear.[84] Actionable guidance for setting awesome habits that compound over time.

- *GRIT* by Angela Duckworth.[85] A compelling book about perseverance and success. The book also contains a 'parenting for GRIT' section.

- *Rich Dad Poor Dad* by Robert Kiyosaki.[86] This book addresses financial education topics with everyday context in terms of income, outgoings, assets and liabilities. It challenges common definitions and aspirations and encourages the reader to apply the teachings to their own view of work and money.

- *Key Person of Influence* by Daniel Priestley.[87] This book introduces the concept of personal brand and holds the secret to setting yourself up as an influential professional in your chosen field to attract higher-value work. It teaches a method by which to make this happen with specific actions at each of the five steps.

To supplement education and prepare students as thinkers, ready to succeed as entrepreneurs, parents need to get their children reading. And not just reading Instagram post captions or texts – reading tough, complex books and articles. This provides a workout for their brains and builds muscles that will help them not only in school, but also in any professional venture, especially as an entrepreneur where one has to build her own path. As Maryanne Wolf's recently released book *Reader,*

Come Home asserts, deep reading is crucial to all of our success – even in the age of technology.

Colette Coleman, Coleman Strategy

When they aren't sure if they'll have what it takes to be in the paper or be the boss, Dr Seuss *Oh the Places You'll Go* never disappoints! ... I'm regularly on the lookout for picture books that share stories of entrepreneurship. A current favorite is *The Most Magnificent Thing* by Ashley Spires. *Lemonade in Winter* by Emily Jenkins is another that introduces the concept of profits as a key measure of business success.

Kimmie Greene, Intuit QuickBooks

From an early age, my parents would make me listen to self-improvement audio courses in order to earn my allowance. Courses from Earl Nightingale, Napoleon Hill, Bob Proctor, Tony Robbins and others were burned into my memory. Most of these authors would promote the concept of being an entrepreneur to control your own destiny and earning potential. It gave me great confidence and a sense of optimism about what I could create.

Carson Conant, Mediafly

OPRAH WINFREY

Known for: Media mogul

What else: She became a billionaire in 2003, and is often ranked as the most influential woman in the world.

When Oprah was born, her father was far away in the army serving at a naval base. Oprah's mother moved to Milwaukee to work as a maid, having left little Oprah on a farm with her strict grandmother. If Oprah misbehaved or did not do what she was ordered to, her grandmother beat her with a stick.

The seclusion of the farm where Oprah was growing up forced her to make up and create her own ways of entertainment. She made friends with household animals and found a friend in books. There was no television on the farm and, according to Oprah, it was her grandmother, Hattie Mae (Presley) Lee, who gave her the most precious gift in life, having taught her to read and write before she even turned three.

Oprah recalls her strict grandmother as her first role model. In an interview, she said that her strength and way of thinking are all the results of her grandmother's work and effort. Every Sunday, Hattie Mae took Oprah to church where people nicknamed Oprah 'The Preacher'. When she was reciting Bible verses in her unique and inimitable manner, people in church stood in awe. Oprah never forgot that early success and made her dream to become a missionary or a preacher. Later her fourth grade teacher, Mrs Duncan, inspired her to become a teacher.

When Oprah started kindergarten at the age of five, she diligently wrote a request letter to her teacher asking to move her straight to the first grade. A surprised teacher did so. Having studied in the first grade, Oprah was then transferred directly to the third.

INSPIRATIONAL SONGS

JODIE

To help me get in the zone for something I'm about to do, I listen to music that elicits a specific response. If I'm writing, I listen to concentration or focus music; before a sports competition it'll be faster paced hype music; and before an important meeting or public speaking gig it'll be music that fills me with confidence and makes me smile. Before bedtime, I make sure it's only soothing sounds and chillout tracks that reach my ears.

Steven Pinker, a cognitive psychologist, labels music an 'auditory cheesecake'.[88] It doesn't create your experience entirely, but it can definitely enhance it. Any parent who has played music on a long car journey will know the different moods that different tracks can evoke, not to mention how long catchy tunes can stick in your head for. ('Baby Shark' anyone?)

At home, the choice of music can set the tone for the time you spend there. The lyrics and beats enter the subconscious and can be happy, motivational and uplifting or exactly the opposite if you're not careful.

I love songs that inspire an 'anything is possible' mindset. Here are some examples we received from parents for you to try in your home or add to a playlist for a certain event:

- 🚀 'Try Everything' by Shakira, from the film *Zootopia*[89]
- 🚀 'Let It Go' from the film *Frozen*[90]
- 🚀 'This Is Me' from the film *The Greatest Showman*[91]
- 🚀 'Firework' by Katy Perry[92]
- 🚀 'Never Give Up' by Sia, from the film *Lion*[93]
- 🚀 'Watch Me Shine' by Joanna Pacitti, from the film *Legally Blonde*[94]

ACTIONABLES

Create feel-good playlists to inspire positivity by:

- ✦ Looking up the lyrics of your children's favourite songs and talking about the messages.
- ✦ Downloading the soundtracks of their favourite films.
- ✦ Talking about how each song makes them feel and separating themes into different playlists.
- ✦ Choosing different categories, for example: a wakeup playlist, a bedtime playlist, a relaxation playlist or one to accompany creative pursuits.
- ✦ Taking turns to add tracks to the playlist or voting on which should be included.

I remember listening to songs 'I believe I can fly', 'We will rock you' and 'Upgrade you'. Now I play classical music in my home when I need to feel relaxed or focused.

Kalina Stoyanova, Independent Fashion Bloggers

We are big fans of the song 'Let it Go' from the movie *Frozen,* and 'Whatever it Takes' by Imagine Dragons. Both have great messages.

Laura Hunter, LashLiner LLC

Growing up in Germany in the 1980s, there were a number of NDW (New German Wave) songs about topics related to entrepreneurship... for example, 'Bruttosozialprodukt' (gross national product) by Geier Sturzflug and 'Der Nippel' (the nipple) by Mike Krüger – basically, a song about user experience.

Sabine Harnau, From Scratch Communications

ESTÉE LAUDER

Known for: Founder of the Estée Lauder Companies Inc

What else: Lauder is thought to have originated the marketing practice of giving a free gift with every purchase.

Estée Lauder (named Josephine Esther Mentzer but nicknamed Estée) was born to Hungarian and Czech Jewish parents and raised in New York.

Lauder's father, Max Mentzer, owned a hardware store in Queens. While attending high school, Lauder worked in this shop, along with most of her eight siblings. Here she learned the basics of retailing; not only about perfectionism, but also about merchandising and promoting quality products. She particularly remembered how they gift-wrapped hammers and nails, which her father gifted to his customers during the Christmas time.

Lauder showed her interest in beauty at an early age. With a determination to look good, she wanted to be a successful actress, with her name and fame known worldwide. She loved to brush her mother's long hair and apply creams to her face.

Shortly after the outbreak of World War I, Estée's maternal uncle, chemist John Schotz, came to live with them. She watched him at work, learned his craft and soon started to make her own beauty creams. Lauder said that her uncle was like 'a magician and mentor'[95] – he captured her imagination like no one else could.

When Lauder was a teenager, she started selling her products at local hair salons, calling them 'jars of hope' and giving out free samples to secure orders.

Lauder was the subject of a 1985 TV documentary, *Estée Lauder: The Sweet Smell of Success*. Explaining her success, she said, 'I have never worked a day in my life without selling. If I believe in something, I sell it and I sell it hard.'[96]

FAMILY MEMBERS

JODIE

There's a British genealogy television show called *Who Do You Think You Are* in which celebrities trace their family trees back, often with surprising results. The guests find out their ancestors went through many challenges and held all sorts of jobs. Some guests have found out their great-great-great-grandparents were convicts, or gang members, or made significant contributions to history within their lifetime.

The show's format has been replicated for many different countries. The concept of someone learning about their ancestors is fascinating and can be recreated at home fairly easily. Because these people share our blood, hearing their stories can help the success they might have found feel attainable and accessible. It can motivate and inspire us. If they experienced hardships, it might give us confidence that we can apply resilience and get through tough times of our own. Whatever is contained within the stories of distant relatives, we can learn from them.

There are so many ways to learn about your family tree. I love hearing stories of my ancestors and what they did. Within my family there are all sorts of stories of people who overcame adversity to get to a better place.

ACTIONABLES

- Search your surname on www.findmypast.co.uk/surname or www.geni.com/surnames.

- Ask aunts, uncles and grandparents about their grandparents and distant relatives and what they know about them. Take notes.

- Keep going until you find a story that resonates.

- Profile family members. Draw them and write their biographies.

- Ask grandparents what they did to earn money and what their biggest achievements were.

- Ask grandparents how they overcame obstacles.

- Use the learning in real-life examples. Ask questions such as, 'How would [family member] have responded to this challenge?'

- Run out of family members? Use examples from history instead. See who sparks an interest and explore their journey and achievements.

If you aren't able to trace your family tree, there are plenty of other ways to find people whose stories your family can learn from:

- Think about everyone you have something in common with. Include people who live on your street, in your town or city, went to the same school as you, even those who support the same soccer team.

- Make a list of those with an interesting story or career.

- Make a plan to talk to them about it as a family.

- Plant the questions and inspire intrigue. 'Ask Mr X about... and ask Mrs Y about...'

- Think beyond the people you actually know. The internet and books can provide a huge source of biographies, and museums all over the world are set up to share the stories of remarkable people, for example: the Anne Frank house, Robben Island where Nelson Mandela spent 18 of his 27 years in prison, and many more.

As a child, my dad talked to me often about my grandfather and although sadly, I never met him, his journey inspired me. My grandfather, Stanley N. Evans served in France and Belgium during the First World War, went on to become a Labour party politician and ran his own successful business. Over the years, whenever I achieved something my dad was proud of, he would say the phrase his father used to say to him, 'Derby winners breed derby winners,' which would make me smile and fill me with confidence that anything was possible!

Sam Taylor, Tinker Taylor

My maternal grandfather arrived in the US at nineteen, bare pocketed, with a connection to the risky Pennsylvania coal mines. His stories of finding his way out of the coal mines and working odd jobs as a butler, gardener and home maintenance man on his way to Cleveland, OH, where he founded his own ironworks that is still in operation inspired me further.

Susan Gold, SGC, LLC

When I was three years old, my mother made the brave decision to free our family from the Vietnam War by escaping to California. Many of the lessons I learned from my mother, including the sacrifices she made and the hardships she endured to protect her family, were taught by example. I recognize and appreciate them so much now as an adult, and they have guided my career direction and are an integral part of my business practices.

Quynh Mai, MI&C

I have been teaching my niece, age three, about amazing women from history and I've taught her about all the amazing women that have come before her. Her hero is now Marie Curie and she wants to be a doctor and help people like Marie Curie did.

Naomi Pryde, DWF LLP

HOWARD SCHULTZ

Known for: Chairman and CEO of Starbucks

What else: In 1988, Starbucks became one of the first companies in America to give health insurance to all its employees – including part-time workers, a benefit that was unheard of at the time.

Schultz was three years old when his family moved into a small apartment in one of Brooklyn's public housing projects, where there was nothing but the concrete basketball and football courts. Schultz always knew how difficult it would be for him to break out of poverty, but his dream of becoming successful was stronger than any obstacle.

From Schultz's website: 'The most indelible image I have of my dad is of him lying on our couch in a cast, distraught. I was about seven years old. It was winter, and he had a job delivering cloth diapers. He'd fallen on a patch of ice and broken his hip and ankle. He was fired from his job and had no health insurance, no workers compensation and no savings. The image of my father on the couch, helpless, stuck with me.

'Most people called my mother Bobbi. She was a fierce believer in the American Dream, and it was my mom who gave me the confidence to believe that I could one day build a better life for myself. Our family rarely had enough money to pay the bills, and there was a lot of angst in our seventh-floor apartment. I escaped the family chaos by sitting in the stairwell between floors and imagining a better life.'[97]

Schultz's first job after college was selling office equipment door-to-door. Each day he made up to fifty cold calls. He liked talking to people, was pretty good at sales, and always gave half of his paycheque to his parents.

LEADING BY EXAMPLE

JODIE

A child can only aspire to be what they know exists. In order for their imagination, and therefore their dreams and aspirations, to be big, they must realise the possibilities. With the entrepreneurs and business leaders we heard from, as well as the founders of many household-name brands, the friends and family members they met when they were small had a profound impact on their ambition and future.

For some, it was understanding the intricacies of another's craft and emulating their precision and determination. For others, it was seeing how someone approached their work and the values they lived by. The chance to meet and understand a variety of people from all walks of life marked multiple points of reference from which someone could form their own goals.

Mirroring is where one person unconsciously imitates the actions, words or attitude of another, and it's common in close friendship groups and families. Mirroring is an act rooted in the need for humans to empathise and build connections and rapport, but its implications might span someone's entire lifespan and affect their career, relationships and mindset.[98]

The people with whom a child interacts will shape the person they become. Someone being intentionally introduced to inspirational, successful and happy people will direct their thoughts and behaviour that way.

Whatever you choose to say and do will be set as the benchmark for acceptable and desirable behaviour, so leading by example is paramount in raising entrepreneurial kids. The other ways outlined in the book pale into insignificance when compared to the power of practising what you preach and being the role model that your children can emulate.

Many entrepreneurs grew up knowing entrepreneurial role models. They had experience of someone who displayed remarkable confidence, positivity, creativity and a problem-solving mindset. Those traits were mirrored, internalised and stayed with them as they began to make their own career choices.

You will be your child's most influential role model. You have the power to give your children the skills and characteristics they'll need to become truly enterprising – from the questions you ask, the values you set and the behaviour you display.

Make it your goal that, in the future, your children are pleased to hear someone comment, 'You sound just like your mum,' or 'You're just like your dad.' Their mannerisms, their attitude and outlook and even their handwriting can be influenced by yours.

ACTIONABLES

Start with you:

- 🚀 What are the habits that you *would* want your kids to mirror and the habits you *wouldn't* want your kids to mirror?
- 🚀 How can you do more of the first and less of the second?
- 🚀 What have you noticed them mirroring already?
- 🚀 How can you take steps to be an amazing role model?
- 🚀 What do you wish you had seen or experienced from a young age?

I think that the most important thing is to lead by example. I tend to work a lot when my kids are around since high-tech is pretty much 24x7, but I think this actually exposes them to values that are important to me, like hard work, seeing things through, taking responsibility and enjoying what you do.

Lisa Bennett, Kaltura

My dad left when I was five years old, leaving my mum with no choice but to work all hours just so she could keep a roof over our heads. To this day she is my inspiration and definitely where I got my 'grafter' work ethic from, that has been the basis of my success in business to date. My mum was a hairdresser, a cleaner at multiple places and a care assistant, sometimes all at the same time! I didn't see her much growing up but I understood what she was doing and why because she explained it to me at the time.

When I was twelve, I went to work on a farm every evening and weekend and school holiday. It was partly because I knew that if I wanted nice things, I would need to earn the money to buy them myself, and partly because I wasn't scared of hard work having seen my mum do it. To this day, in running my own business, I put my work ethic and entrepreneurial drive down to my mum leading by example.

Lee Gill, Flow Office Furniture and Interiors

My mother was one of the first three women who graduated from Boston University law school, and on full scholarship. She taught me that success doesn't come easy and it's only through the hardest dedication and persistence that one can be successful.

David Stone, Forager

JEFF BEZOS

Known for: Founder and CEO of Amazon

What else: The richest man in the world and on track to become the first trillionaire by 2026.

Described today as 'hyper-intelligent, ultra-driven, and obsessed with detail',[99] Bezos showed an early interest in how things work. As a toddler, he managed to dismantle his crib with a screwdriver. As a teen, his younger sister and brother loved going into their brother's room because of all the fascinating toys, so he developed an electric alarm to alert him of their approach.

When Bezos was twelve, he wanted something called an Infinity Cube. The device was a set of small motorised mirrors that reflected off one another so the images seemed to go on endlessly. It cost $20 but Bezos did not have enough money to buy it. Instead, he purchased mirrors and other parts with the money he had and constructed his own reflecting cube.

Bezos's parents eventually asked him to move all his inventions to their garage, which he converted into a laboratory for his science projects. Bezos attended elementary school in Houston from fourth to sixth grade. He would spend summers at the ranch working on tasks such as laying pipe, fixing windmills, vaccinating cattle and other farm work.

While Bezos was in high school, he worked at McDonald's as a short-order line cook during the breakfast shift. He started his first business, The DREAM Institute, at school. It was an educational summer camp for fourth, fifth and sixth graders.

His grandfather was a role model in his life, with his wide-ranging knowledge of science and constant presence on the ranch. In a 2010 commencement speech at Princeton University, Bezos told graduates that his grandfather taught him how 'it's harder to be kind than clever.'[100]

OUTRO

DANIEL

Do you remember that squishy little face and tiny little body that so rapidly transformed into a curious little kid? Have you noticed how quickly kids become taller and ganglier? One minute they're crawling, then walking, then suddenly they're engaging you in a debate. Little children transform into adolescents at warp speed, and then they are off into the world to make their mark as young adults.

If you're reading a book like this, you've probably already shared thousands of empowering little moments with your kid. No doubt you've deliberately taken time to steer them in the right direction amid all the important things you're already doing just to provide a home – moments when your words and actions shape them for the better.

Being a parent is tough work, even providing the basics of life these days can be challenging for many people at times. Going above and beyond to provide unique mentoring, skills and opportunities isn't a small thing, but it's important – not just for your kids, but also for you. When you get them to try something new and learn a valuable lesson, when you challenge them, trick them or even bribe them to step outside their comfort zone, you open the door for them to discover their own creativity, influence and power.

What if it turned out that one of these moments was your most important life's work? If between all of your pressures and demands, something you said or did got through to them and set them on an important path? What if a small gesture from you piqued their curiosity, gave them confidence, taught them a skill or got them thinking in a more resourceful way?

What if it snowballed and your child ended up making some great choices in their twenties, doing important work in their thirties, and creating something hugely valuable to contribute to the world?

It's possible that the small things you do today are going to become really big things someday. The biggest achievements in your career may become small by comparison and your most important achievement may be to have raised a confident, capable and compassionate human being.

The world's most iconic entrepreneurs and change-makers often recall memories from their childhood that set them on the path to success and influence. Baroness Michelle Mone OBE grew up in poverty in a rough part of Scotland but went on to become a multi-millionaire with the success of her impressive Ultimo lingerie business. She recalls words of encouragement from her grandmother in a Chinese restaurant that made her feel she could break out of her impoverished circumstances and shoot for the stars. Today, she's on the board of important charities and is a Baroness in the House of Lords, shaping policy that will impact millions of lives.

Michelle's granny didn't get a big cheque, an OBE or a peerage in the House of Lords but she made all the difference when it mattered. Her mentoring over that bowl of Chinese food set forth a chain of events that improved the world.

Self-made billionaire Bhavin Turakhia says that his father told him hundreds of times, 'You can do anything you set your mind to, so long as it doesn't break the fundamental laws of physics.'[101] That advice, combined with a $350 loan, led to a global business, a family fortune and inspiration to thousands of entrepreneurs. *Forbes* magazine hasn't put Bhavin's father on the cover, but without him there wouldn't be his billionaire son. Installing the right mental software came long before the valuable software company.

Richard Branson constantly talks about the role his mother Eve played in his upbringing. He credits his childhood experiences in setting him on a path to disrupting dozens of industries, creating thousands of good jobs and influencing millions of people. It's Sir Richard Branson who will be remembered as one of the greatest entrepreneurs and change-makers of all time, but he is the first to say that he simply wouldn't have gotten started if it wasn't for the go-getter moxie his mother fostered in him.

Contained within the stories in this book, you've seen hundreds of ways that entrepreneurial kids from all walks of life were raised.

You've seen strategies for shifting children's mindsets towards creativity, empathy, strategy, mastery, resilience and freedom.

Now more than ever, the world needs leaders who can get big things done. Humanity has toxic societal issues, we are dangerously close to irreversibly damaging our habitat, we are pumping chemicals into the air, dumping plastic into our oceans, and distributing resources in ways that do not serve more than half the people on earth.

We know the problems facing humanity. The United Nations has defined its seventeen sustainable development goals (SDGs) that focus on major issues that impact billions of lives, vast ecosystems, or our own survival as a species.

Whilst this book proudly supports goal numbers 4: quality education; 8: decent work and economic growth; and 10: reduced inequalities; each of the seventeen problems is also an opportunity waiting for someone to come up with a scalable and valuable solution that investors and markets can get behind.

As a parent or guardian, I'm sure you can't help noticing these issues. Sadly, all of these problems won't be fixed by the time your kids go out into the world, but they can be solved with good leadership and creative thinking. The world needs more people who can solve meaningful problems at scale. The world needs people who can craft ideas into action and create something valuable. The world needs creative rebels, change-makers, compassionate leaders and innovative entrepreneurs.

At its core, entrepreneurship is about solving problems at scale. By raising entrepreneurial kids, you're laying the foundations for a future leader to emerge who will be empowered to improve the world in some way. The goal is not to make your kids into child-entrepreneurs – it's to give them confidence, skills and opportunities that will lead to them being adults who can change things.

In the past 100 years, the best opportunities related to making sporting shoes, setting up burger restaurants or putting personal computers in everyone's homes or pockets. Those opportunities are now mature and highly saturated. The best opportunities in the next 100 years will be about solving the problems we face as a planet. We're going to see billionaires made through sustainable energy, removing plastic waste, inventing new food production methods, reinventing education and ending poverty.

The term legacy is often confused. Many people think of their legacy as how they will be remembered. In truth, few people are remembered, no matter what they did or who they were. There are plenty of kings, queens, prime ministers and presidents who are hardly remembered today. If they aren't remembered, what chance do most of us have?

The true meaning of the term legacy is to pass something on. Passing on your knowledge, your experiences and your insights is how to create a legacy and it's possible for anyone. Maybe you won't be remembered but your efforts will have a ripple effect through time.

It's entirely possible that a kid you raised will go on to make a dent in the universe in ways you can hardly imagine right now.

Your legacy could well be less about what you achieve and more about what your kids achieve as a result of your thoughtful parenting style. This book is just the beginning.

We hope you loved this book, and we can't wait to hear how it makes a difference.

Visit clevertykes.com/book for further reading, resources and inspiration, and to:

- Take the scorecard
- Submit your story
- Find the accompanying playbook
- Receive entrepreneurial stories straight to your inbox
- Watch interviews with the authors
- Join the Facebook community
- Access free downloads and exclusive material

NOTES

PART ONE

1. Morrow, D, 'Excerpts From an Oral History Interview with Lawrence Ellison, President and CEO Oracle Corporation', Smithsonian Institution Oral and Video Histories, 1995, https://americanhistory.si.edu/comphist/le1.html, accessed 5 August 2020

2. Farzan, A, 'From A College Dropout To A $54 Billion Fortune', Business Insider, 2015, www.businessinsider.com/rags-to-riches-story-of-larry-ellison-2015-5?r=US&IR=T, accessed 20 October 2020

3. Kiyosaki, R, *Rich Dad Poor Dad* (Plata Publishing, Second edition, 2017)

4. Collinson, P, 'One in Three UK Millennials Will Never Own a Home', *The Guardian*, 2018, www.theguardian.com/money/2018/apr/17/one-in-three-uk-millennials-will-never-own-a-home-report, accessed 5 August 2020

5. Quin, M, 'UK Personal Debt Levels Continue to Rise', 2018, www.moneyexpert.com/debt/uk-personal-debt-levels-continue-rise, accessed 5 August 2020

6. Guest Writer, 'All About Esther Afua Ocloo: A successful businesswoman', Scoop Empire, 2020, https://scoopempire.com/all-about-esther-afua-ocloo-a-successful-businesswoman, accessed 5 August 2020

7. Durant, W, *The Story of Philosophy* (Pocket Books, Second edition, January 1991)

8. Itzler, J, *Living with a SEAL: 31 days training with the toughest man on the planet* (Center Street, Reprint edition, January 2017)

9. Cook, J, 'Season 1, Episode 16: Carrie Green, founder of the Female Entrepreneur Association' [podcast], Creating Useful People, 2016, http://podcast.clevertykes.com/204516/1856704-carrie-green-founder-of-the-female-entrepreneur-association, accessed 4 August 2020

10. Feloni, R, '"Shark Tank" Investor Daymond John Explains How His Mom Helped FUBU Become A $350 Million Company', Business Insider, 2015, finance.yahoo.com/news/shark-tank-investor-daymond-john-180122915.html, accessed 20 October 2020

11. Blanco, O, 'Daymond John on Hip-Hop, His Mom and Making It Big', CNN Money, https://money.cnn.com/interactive/economy/my-american-success-story-daymond-john/index.html, accessed 6 August 2020

12. Tan, S Y, and Yip, A, 'Hans Selye (1907–1982): Founder of the stress theory', 2018, *Singapore Med J*, 59(4): 170–71, www.ncbi.nlm.nih.gov/pmc/articles/PMC5915631, accessed 4 August 2020

13. Chris Gardner website, www.chrisgardnermedia.com/biography, accessed 6 August 2020

14. Yang, J, '"Happyness" For Sale: He's gone from homeless single dad to successful stockbroker', CNN Money, 2006, https://money.cnn.com/magazines/fortune/fortune_archive/2006/09/18/8386184/index.htm, accessed 6 August 2020

15. Gordon, D, 'Chris Gardner: The homeless man who became a multi-millionaire investor', *Business Reporter*, December 2016, www.bbc.co.uk/news/business-38144980, accessed 5 August 2020

16. Created by Amin Toufani, www.adaptability.org

17. Fratto, N, '3 Ways to Measure Your Adaptability – and How to Improve' [TED talk], May 2019, www.ted.com/talks/natalie_fratto_3_ways_to_measure_your_adaptability_and_how_to_improve_it/transcript?language=en, accessed 5 August 2020

18. Razak, A, and Rossi, A, 'An Investigation into the Micro-dynamics of Routine Flexibility', Semantic Scholar, 2017, www.semanticscholar.org/paper/An-investigation-into-the-micro-dynamics-of-routine-Razak-Rossi/17db3f5556169053a16d4643fc103b02c96ddd13

19. Strauss, N, 'Elon Musk: The architect of tomorrow', *Rolling Stone*, 2017, www.rollingstone.com/culture/culture-features/elon-musk-the-architect-of-tomorrow-120850, accessed 5 August 2020

20. Suter, A, 'Elon Musk – The Tech Genius and His Visions for the Future Avatar', Techstory, 2018, https://techstory.in/elon-musk-tech-genius/, accessed 5 August 2020

21. Seuss, Dr, *Happy Birthday to You!* (Random House, 1959)

22. www.twainquotes.com/Majority.html, directory of Mark Twain's maxims, quotations and various opinions, accessed 6 August 2020

23. Stych, A, 'Self-checkouts Contribute to Retail Jobs Decline', Bizwomen, 2019, www.bizjournals.com/bizwomen/news/latest-news/2019/04/self-checkouts-contribute-to-retail-jobs-decline.html?page=all, accessed 6 August 2020

24. Hawkins, A, 'Uber is Bringing Its Self-driving Cars to Dallas', The Verge, 2019, www.theverge.com/2019/9/17/20870969/uber-self-driving-car-testing-dallas, accessed 6 August 2020

25. Frey, C B, and Osborne, M, 'Working Paper: The future of employment', Oxford Martin Programme on Technology and Employment, 2013, www.oxfordmartin.ox.ac.uk/downloads/academic/future-of-employment.pdf, accessed 6 August 2020

26. Branson, R, 'My Mother's Unconventional Parenting Lessons', Virgin.com, 2016, www.virgin.com/richard-branson/my-mothers-unconventional-parenting-lessons, accessed 6 August 2020

27. Ferriss, T, *Tools of Titans: The tactics, routines, and habits of billionaires, icons, and world-class performers* (Vermilion, First edition, 2016)

28. Ferriss, T, 'Real Mind Control: The 21-day no-complaint experiment' [blog], 2017, https://tim.blog/2007/09/18/real-mind-control-the-21-day-no-complaint-experiment

29. McKay, B, et al., 'Never Complain; Never Explain' [blog], Art Of Manliness, 2016, www.artofmanliness.com/articles/never-complain-never-explain, accessed 5 August 2020

PART TWO

30. Kelly, K, '68 Bits of Unsolicited Advice' [blog], The Technium, 2020, https://kk.org/thetechnium/68-bits-of-unsolicited-advice/?mc_cid=32f8068abf&mc_eid=5b1af35cae, accessed 4 August 2020

31. Altucher, J, *Choose Yourself!* (CreateSpace Independent Publishing Platform, 2013)

32. Cook, J, 'Season 1, Episode 17: Sara Davies' [podcast], Creating Useful People, 2019, http://podcast.clevertykes.com/204516/2148512-sara-davies-founder-of-crafter-s-companion

33. Huffington, A, *Thrive* (WH Allen, 2015)

34. Kidder, D, 'How Spanx Came to Be: A girl was allowed to sit and think', Quartz, 2013, https://qz.com/65713/how-spanx-came-to-be-a-girl-was-allowed-to-sit-and-think, accessed 5 August 2020

35. Loudenback, T, 'Spanx Founder Sara Blakely Learned an Important Lesson About Failure From Her Dad – Now She's Passing It on to Her 4 Kids', Business Insider, 2018, www.businessinsider.com/spanx-founder-sara-blakely-redefine-failure-2016-10?r=UK, accessed 5 August 2020

36. PPC Evolved, 'Phone Anxiety Affects Over Half of UK Office Workers', 2019, https://ffb.co.uk/blog/630-phone-anxiety-affects-over-half-of-uk-office-workers, accessed 6 August 2020

37. Chapelton, T, 'How Can Young Children Best Learn Languages?', The British Council, 2016, www.britishcouncil.org/voices-magazine/how-can-young-children-best-learn-languages, accessed 6 August 2020

38. 'Jack Ma', *Forbes*, www.forbes.com/profile/jack-ma/?list=rtb/#4732e5f91ee4, accessed 6 August 2020

39. Stone, M, et al, 'Jack Ma is Resigning From SoftBank's Board', Business Insider, 2020, www.businessinsider.com/inspiring-life-story-of-alibaba-founder-jack-ma-2017-2?r=US&IR=T, accessed 6 August 2020

40. Associated Press, 'The World Health Organization Says If Your Baby is Younger Than 1 Year Old, They Should Spend No Time in Front of Your Smartphone', Business Insider, 2019, www.businessinsider.com/world-health-organization-releases-new-screen-time-guidance-for-babies-2019-4, accessed 6 August 2020

41. Akhtar, A, et al., 'Bill Gates and Steve Jobs Raised Their Kids with Limited Tech – and It Should Have Been a Red Flag About Our Own Smartphone Use', Business Insider, 2020, www.businessinsider.com/screen-time-limits-bill-gates-steve-jobs-red-flag-2017-10?r=US&IR=T, accessed 6 August 2020

42. Andersson, H, 'Social Media Apps Are "Deliberately" Addictive to Users', BBC Panorama, 2018, www.bbc.co.uk/news/technology-44640959, accessed 6 August 2020

43. Altucher, J, '20 Things I've Learned From Larry Page', 2015, Medium, https://medium.com/the-mission/20-things-i-ve-learned-from-larry-page-4f83674a1a52, accessed 6 August 2020

44. Page, L, 'Want to Change the World? Have Fun', Newsroom, 2018, www.morningfuture.com/en/article/2018/03/30/larry-page-google-work-future-innovation/262, accessed 6 August 2020

45. Kishimi, I, *The Courage to Be Disliked: How to free yourself, change your life and achieve real happiness* (Allen & Unwin, 2019)

46. Fisher, R, and Ury, W, *Getting to Yes: Negotiating an agreement without giving in* (Random House Business, 2012)

47. 'The Battle for the Orange', The Compasito Manual On Human Rights Education For Children, Chapter 4, www.eycb.coe.int/compasito/chapter_4/4_30.asp

48. Vaynerchuk, G, 'How to Give Your Kids Confidence and Self-Esteem' [video], 2019, www.facebook.com/gary/videos/vb.51535068349/309689463040557/?type=2&theater, accessed 6 August 2020

49. Gary Vaynerchuk website, www.garyvaynerchuk.com/for-tamara-and-all-the-other-moms, accessed 6 August 2020

50. Stangor, C, *Principles of Social Psychology*, 2012, https://opentextbc.ca/socialpsychology

51. 'A Framework for Character Education in Schools', The Jubilee Centre for Character & Virtues, 2017, www.jubileecentre.ac.uk/userfiles/jubileecentre/pdf/character-education/Framework%20for%20Character%20Education.pdf

52. 'Amancio Ortega Gaona Biography: Success story of Zara co-founder', Astrum People, https://astrumpeople.com/amancio-ortega-gaona-biography, accessed 6 August 2020

PART THREE

53. 'Mark Zuckerberg Biography (1984–)', Biography, 2019, www.biography.com/business-figure/mark-zuckerberg, accessed 6 August 2020

54. Murphy Jr, B, 'Want to Raise Entrepreneurial Kids? Mark Zuckerberg's Dad Says Do These Things', Inc., www.inc.com/bill-murphy-jr/want-to-raise-entrepreneurial-kids-mark-zuckerbergs-dad-says-do-these-things.html, accessed 6 August 2020

55. Wai, J, 'The Chess Concepts Peter Thiel Used to Become a Billionaire', Business Insider, 2012, www.businessinsider.com/the-chess-concepts-that-taught-peter-thiel-how-to-become-a-billionaire-2012-6?r=US&IR=T, accessed 6 August 2020

56. Gilliland, J, 'Hershey, Milton Snavely', American National Biography, 1999, www.anb.org/view/10.1093/anb/9780198606697.001.0001/anb-9780198606697-e-1000772;jsessionid=4CBC321B4C50CDD4109A7FD1553D53EA, accessed 6 August 2020

57. Chappelow, J, 'Keynesian Economics', Investopedia, www.investopedia.com/terms/k/keynesianeconomics.asp, accessed 5 August 2020

58. Cook, J, 'Season 1 Episode 9: Deepak Tailor, founder of LatestFreeStuff. co.uk' [podcast], Creating Useful People, 2018, http://podcast.clevertykes. com/204516/808702-deepak-tailor-founder-of-latestfreestuff-co-uk, accessed 4 August 2020

59. 'Ingvar Kamprad Biography: Success story of IKEA founder', Astrum People, https://astrumpeople.com/ingvar-kamprad-biography-success-story-of-ikea-founder, accessed 6 August 2020

60. 'Ingvar Kamprad Biography: Success story of IKEA founder', Astrum People, https://astrumpeople.com/ingvar-kamprad-biography-success-story-of-ikea-founder, accessed 6 August 2020

61. Aughtmon, S, 'IKEA Founder on the Value of 10 Minutes (Motivational Business Quotes)', Bay Business Help, 2018, https://baybusinesshelp.com/2018/01/08/ ikea-founder-on-the-value-of-10-minutes-motivational-business-quotes, accessed 6 August 2020

62. Allcott, G, *How to Be a Productivity Ninja: Worry less, achieve more and love what you do* (Icon Books, Second edition, 2016)

63. 'John Paul Dejoria', *Forbes*, www.forbes.com/profile/john-paul-dejoria/#3fd5396224a4, accessed 6 August 2020

64. 'John Paul Dejoria: From homeless single father to billionaire', Anisometric, 2019, www.anisometric-inc.com/john-paul-dejoria-from-homeless-single-father-to-billionaire, accessed 6 August 2020

PART FOUR

65. 'Jack Dorsey Biography: Success story of Twitter co-founder', Astrum People, https://astrumpeople.com/jack-dorsey-biography-success-story-of-twitter-co-founder, accessed 6 August 2020

66. Jack Dorsey, 'The Innovator' [video], 2013, www.youtube.com/ watch?v=eKHoTOYTFH8&t=7s, accessed 4 August 2020

67. 'How Would the Person I Would Like to Be, Do the Things I'm About to Do?', Female Entrepreneur Association, https://femaleentrepreneurassociation. com/2012/04/how-would-the-person-i-would-like-to-be-do-the-things-im-about-to-do, accessed 4 August 2020

68. 'Top 20 Thomas Edison Quotes to Motivate You to Never Quit', Goalcast, 2017, www.goalcast.com/2017/05/11/thomas-edison-quotes-motivate-never-quit, accessed 6 August 2020

69. Haralabidou, A, 'The Philosophy of Epic Entrepreneurs: Thomas Edison & the Vagabonds', Virgin, October 2015, www.virgin.com/entrepreneur/philosophy-epic-entrepreneurs-thomas-edison-vagabonds, accessed 5 August 2020

70. Young, V, 'Jo Malone – "I'm Still the Girl That Made Good"', Woman and Home, October 2016, www.womanandhome.com/life/books/exclusive-jo-malone-i-m-still-the-girl-that-made-good-65359, accessed 5 August 2020

71. 'Jo Malone Biography', Encyclopaedia of World Biography, www.notablebiographies.com/newsmakers2/2004-Ko-Pr/Malone-Jo.html, accessed 6 August 2020

72. Shpancer, N, 'What Doesn't Kill You Makes You Weaker', Psychology Today, 2010, www.psychologytoday.com/gb/blog/insight-therapy/201008/what-doesnt-kill-you-makes-you-weaker#:~:text=Friedrich%20Nietzsche%2C%20the%20German%20philosopher,to%20resonate%20within%20American%20culture, accessed 5 August 2020

73. Wherry, J, 'The Influence of Home on School Success', NAESP.org, 2004, www.naesp.org/sites/default/files/resources/2/Principal/2004/S-Op6.pdf, accessed 5 August 2020

74. Sheils, J, *The Family Board Meeting: You have 18 summers to create lasting connection with your children* (18 Summers Media, August 2018)

75. 'Charlie "Tremendous" Jones', Tremendous Leadership, https://tremendousleadership.com/pages/charlie, accessed 5 August 2020

76. McBratney, S, *Guess How Much I Love You* (Walker Books, 1994)

77. Martin, E W, *The Wonderful Things You'll Be* (Random House Books, 2015)

78. Seuss, Dr, *Oh, the Places You'll Go* (Random House Books, Illustrated edition, 1990)

79. The Clever Tykes series, (JayBee Media Limited, 2014)

80. Syed, M, *You Are Awesome* (Wren & Rook, 2018)

81. Robbins, A, *Awaken the Giant Within* (Simon & Schuster, 1992)

82. Ferriss, T, *4-Hour Work Week* (Harmony, Updated edition, 2009)

83. Gerber, M, *The E-Myth Revisited* (HarperBusiness, 2004)

84. Clear, J, *Atomic Habits* (Avery, 2018)

85. Duckworth, A, *GRIT* (Scribner, 2016)

86. Kiyosaki, R, *Rich Dad Poor Dad* (Plata Publishing, Updated edition, 2017)

87. Priestley, D, *Key Person of Influence* (Rethink Press, Updated edition, 2020)

88. Houri, S, 'Why is Music So Powerful?', Medium, 2018, https://medium.com/the-ascent/why-is-music-so-powerful-e9dc8cf26607, accessed 5 August 2020

89. 'Try Everything' by Shakira, written by Furler, S, Hermansen, T, and Eriksen, M, 2016, Walt Disney

90. 'Let It Go' by Idina Menzel, written by Anderson-Lopez, K, and Lopez, R, 2014, Walt Disney

91. 'This Is Me' by Keala Settle and The Greatest Showman ensemble, written by Pasek, B, and Paul, J, 2017, Atlantic

92. 'Firework' by Katy Perry, written by Perry, K, Eriksen, M, Hermansen, E, et al., 2010, Capitol

93. 'Never Give Up' by Sia, written by Furler, S, and Kurstin, G, 2016, Monkey Puzzle

94. 'Watch Me Shine' by Joanna Pacitti, produced by Dino (Dean Esposito), 2001.

95. Haralabidou, A, 'The Philosophy of Epic Entrepreneurs: Estée Lauder', Virgin, 2015, www.virgin.com/entrepreneur/philosophy-epic-entrepreneurs-estee-lauder, accessed 5 August 2020

96. Haralabidou, A, 'The Philosophy of Epic Entrepreneurs: Estée Lauder', Virgin, 2015, www.virgin.com/entrepreneur/philosophy-epic-entrepreneurs-estee-lauder, accessed 5 August 2020

97. Howard Schultz website, www.howardschultz.com/my-story, accessed 5 August 2020

98. Shellenbarger, S, 'Use Mirroring to Connect with Others', *Wall Street Journal*, 2016, https://www.wsj.com/articles/use-mirroring-to-connect-with-others-1474394329, accessed 5 August 2020

99. 'Jeff Bezos Biography and Success Story | Richest Man On Earth', TNN, 2020, www.trendingnetnepal.com/jeff-bezos-biography, accessed 5 August 2020

100. Sun, C, 'Jeff Bezos: 9 remarkable choices that shaped the richest man in the world', Entrepreneur Europe, 2018, www.entrepreneur.com/slideshow/307224, accessed 5 August 2020

101. Interview with Daniel Priestley

ACKNOWLEDGMENTS

The authors would like to thank the hundreds of parents and entre-preneurs that generously submitted their stories for inclusion in this book.

Whilst we couldn't include all of them, they are very much appreciated.

Thanks to our networks for the support and encouragement at every stage of this venture.

Thank you to the team at Rethink Press for your belief and work in turning our words and ideas into the book you now hold in your hands, with the power to change a lot of lives.

THE AUTHORS

Daniel

Daniel Priestley founded his first company in 2002 in Australia at the age of twenty-one. Before he was twenty-five, he and his business partners had grown a national business turning over several million dollars.

In 2006, Daniel moved from Australia to launch a new venture in London. Arriving with only a suitcase and a credit card, Daniel set up a new venture and grew it to seven-figure revenues in under two years. In the process, he became a leading figure in his industry and is now regarded as one of the world's top professional speakers on business and entrepreneurship.

His business, Dent, reinvents traditional businesses using a unique approach to personal branding and technology.

Daniel is also the author of the books *Key Person of Influence, Entrepreneur Revolution* and *Oversubscribed*. Find Daniel at www.dent.global

Jodie

Jodie Cook founded JC Social Media, an award-winning team of social media managers and trainers based in the United Kingdom, in 2011.

She now writes books and articles on entrepreneurship, happiness and social media. These include *Stop Acting Like You're Going To Live Forever* and its accompanying guided journal, and a children's storybook series, Clever Tykes, which gives entrepreneurial role models to 6–9 year olds. You can find her writing at www.jodiecook.com/writer.

Jodie was included in *Forbes's* '30 under 30 Social Entrepreneurs' in Europe 2017 and in 2017 gave a TEDx talk 'Creating Useful People' at TEDx Aston University. She's a competitive powerlifter and loves to explore the world working remotely. Find Jodie at www.jodiecook.com

www.ingramcontent.com/pod-product-compliance
Lightning Source LLC
Chambersburg PA
CBHW060649150426
42813CB00052B/478